P9-BJE-351

# BOWLING

# About the authors

Joan Martin has taught bowling at the University of Wisconsin and at the University of California at Los Angeles for twenty years. She has been a league bowler and has participated as a special lecturer not only in various bowling clinics sponsored by Lifetime Sports but also in many school clinics in the Los Angeles area. Besides having been a successful coach of this universally popular activity, she has contributed to the literature in the *Research Quarterly* of the American Alliance of Health, Physical Education, and Recreation, and in the *Journal of Sports Medicine*.

Ruth Tandy first taught bowling in an antiquated facility with "grooved" lanes and no pinsetters. Since then she has taught bowling at the Ohio State University lanes, and at the Texas Woman's University where she is currently the coach of the bowling team and a teacher at both the undergraduate and graduate levels. She is active in the National Association for Girls and Women's Sports, in sports officiating, and has served on the national rating and examination boards and the rules committees of several sports activities.

# BOWLING

Physical Education Activities Series

**Joan L. Martin**
University of California, Los Angeles

Revised with

**Ruth E. Tandy**
Texas Woman's University, Denton

THIRD EDITION

Wm C Brown Company Publishers
Dubuque, Iowa

**Consulting Editor**

Aileene Lockhart
Texas Woman's University

**Evaluation Materials Editor**

Jane A. Mott
Smith College

Copyright © 1966, 1971, 1975 by Wm. C. Brown Company Publishers

Library of Congress Catalog Card Number: 74-27899

ISBN 0—697—07060—3

All rights reserved. No part of this publication may be reproduced, stored in a retrieval system, or transmitted, in any form or by any means, electronic, mechanical, photocopying, recording, or otherwise, without the prior written permission of the copyright owner.

Printed in the United States of America

# Contents

# Preface

Bowling is rapidly becoming the leading participating sport for Americans of all ages—teenagers, college students, family groups, and senior citizens. This book is designed to assist these eager enthusiasts, particularly the students, in learning the basic skills and knowledges which lead to optimum bowling performance and pleasure.

There is no substitute for good instruction in the learning process, but good instruction also profits from reinforcement by the written word and visual cues. Most of today's students seek and appreciate opportunities to find out more and more about what they are attempting to learn or do. They require an explanation of the "why" and the "when" as well as the "how to."

The material to be presented delves into all aspects of the game including its early history and development, values, popularity, official rules, scoring, etiquette, bowling language, equipment, and facilities.

Although the emphasis is primarily on instructive material for the novice, the experienced bowler will discover many helpful hints to assist him in correcting faults in his approach or delivery, and adjusting to differences in lane conditions, with some thoughts on strategies and points of concentration for competitive bowling.

Self-evaluation and competency-based questions are distributed throughout this text. These afford the reader typical examples of the kinds of understanding and levels of skill that he should be acquiring as he progresses toward proficiency in bowling. The player should not only answer the printed questions but should pose additional ones as a self-check on learning.

In some instances the student may find that he cannot respond fully and accurately to a question until he has read more extensively or has gained more playing experience. From time to time he should return to such troublesome questions until he is sure of the answers or has developed the skills called for, as the case may be.

Many generous friends, colleagues, and students assisted in the preparation of the manuscript, photographs, and illustrations. My deepest gratitude to Dr. Ruth Abernathy for editing the manuscript, to Jeff Must and Peggy Iden for their assistance in photography and typing, to Ann Stutts for the illustrations, and to Don Sawyer, director of the Student Union Bowling Lanes for his cooperation and valuable suggestions.

My sincere thanks and appreciation to the kind and patient students who performed so well for the photographs: Sam Thompson, Lynne Schwab, Kathy Korda; and to Mike DeAngelo for his cooperation in our use of the lanes and equipment.

I am also indebted to the American Bowling Congress, the Women's International Bowling Congress, AMF and Brunswick, and the National Bowling Council, for supplying us with pertinent information and materials.

My sincerest appreciation is also extended to Ruth E. Tandy, with whom the present revision was accomplished.

JOAN MARTIN

# What bowling is like

1

## PURPOSE OF THE GAME

Bowling appears to consist of the very simple maneuver of rolling a large, heavy ball down a wooden lane at a grouping of ten wooden pins set up in triangular formation at the end of the lane. But bowling, as a game, is deceptive; it calls for a high degree of proficiency, challenging to the most skillful, yet it interests everyone. The object of the game is to knock down as many pins as possible in ten frames. Each frame involves one or two attempts (the tenth frame may involve three attempts). The score is the total number of pins knocked down in the ten frames (plus bonuses). A perfect game of 300 is scored by knocking down all pins with the first ball rolled in each frame ("strike") with two additional balls allowed for a strike in the tenth frame. A low score in the 70s or 80s may result if an inexperienced bowler needs two balls in each frame, very seldom knocks down all the pins in the two attempts, and receives no bonuses for strikes or spares.

A team for league competition consists of four or five bowlers. Systems of handicapping make equalized competition possible.

## VALUES

Bowling has gained respectability and prestige within the past thirty years, to such a degree that it has become one of the most popular sports for participants of all ages, regardless of sex, size, shape, or physical condition (it has, in fact, recently been undertaken by the physically handicapped). Due largely to the effective promotional and supervisorial efforts of the American Bowling Congress, bowling has graduated from a sport of "bums" to a sport of kings, queens, and also just plain folks.

Bowling is not a strenuous game; physical strength is not a limiting factor, and anyone can bowl inexpensively. Most bowling centers today furnish balls free, rent shoes at a nominal fee, and may also furnish free instruction in the fundamentals. The skills used in bowling are not too complicated for average performance and enjoyment. Bowling requires less time in preparation and in actual participation than do golf, skiing, swimming, riding, etc., considerations that make it an excellent activity for a busy family get-together, especially since time is such a limiting factor in the tempo of modern living.

The informal nature of the game allows for socializing and chit-chat between turns; in addition, league bowling affords an opportunity to make many new friends and acquaintances as teams meet different opponents each week.

The time between turns which permits relaxation and socializing is balanced by the need for real concentration and mental alertness in order to judge certain pin formations and strategies of the game when your turn comes along. Bowling offers a constant challenge and watching one's own ball control and average improve can be a great personal satisfaction whether you are bowling informally with family or in a highly competitive league.

Although bowling is not a strenuous activity, it nevertheless demands enough physical exertion to be classified as an enjoyable moderate exercise and it helps in maintaining fitness. It is a safe sport and the probability of injury is slight.


## POPULARITY

That bowling is one of the most popular indoor sports today is evidenced by the fact that over a billion dollars is spent on bowling every year by over fifty million participants. A rapid growth in this sport has taken place since 1954. Increased facilities, automatic pinsetters, and free lessons have made it a sport that is more available than ever to all age groups.

As a service to increase the youth fitness program and to add more carry-over skills to physical education classes, one of the leading bowling manufacturers has developed a "Learn to Bowl" kit for instructor's use in the gymnasium. More than three million students have thus far learned to bowl, and it is expected that eventually 15 million will be reached by this service. College student union buildings are adding bowling facilities to provide recreation and league competition for students, faculty, and employees.

Fig. 1.1.   Everybody Bowls (Courtesy of Brunswick Corporation)

The American Bowling Congress, the Women's International Bowling Congress, and the American Junior Bowling Congress have stimulated interest in bowling by offering free instruction and competitive events for men, women, and young bowlers. Volunteer workers from these organizations donate their time to teach bowling and to organize and conduct leagues.

Television has been a boon to bowling; it has helped to interest thousands of TV sports watchers and has encouraged them to learn the game. The televised tournaments and money matches have encouraged many

Fig. 1.2. Modern Bowling Center (Courtesy of Brunswick Corporation)

skilled bowlers to turn "pro." TV has helped to spread enthusiasm for the sport and has greatly supplemented the promotional efforts of the American Bowling Congress. The pro bowlers have not yet reached the money ranks of the pro golfers, but they are getting there. The leading pros, both men from the Professional Bowlers Association and women from the Professional Woman's Bowlers Association, who bowl on the tournament trail and on television and who sponsor products may earn upwards of $50,000 a year. The average prize money for first place in a bowling tournament is $4,000-$7,000 for men and $1,300-$2,000 for women.

## EQUIPMENT

A unique feature about bowling is that you can learn and can develop a taste for the game without purchasing any equipment. As previously mentioned, most bowling centers rent shoes for a nominal fee and furnish a variety of balls from which you can select one suitable for learning purposes. If you wish to take up bowling in earnest, you should purchase a ball and have it custom-fitted to your hand and grip. Details for the purchase of personal equipment will be found in chapter 9.

Most commercial lanes charge sixty to ninety cents per line, depending on the locale, the spaciousness of the establishment, and the services offered by the proprietor. Original construction outlay, over $18,500 per lane, and the high maintenance costs of keeping the lanes and pin machines in top shape necessitate higher fees in some areas.

A regulation lane or alley consists of the approach, which is a minimum of 15 feet in length and extends to the foul line; the foul line dividing the approach and the alley bed; and the alley bed itself which extends from the foul line 63 feet to the pit end where the pins are set down and removed by the automatic machines. The channels at either side of the alley bed which catch misdirected balls, the ball return, and the rack are also parts of a complete lane.

Regulation lanes are constructed of maple and pine boards set on edge in order to make a solid, durable surface which will withstand much wear. The first 12 to 15 feet of the lane are maple; the pine boards, which are a softer and more porous wood, are used from the "range finder" area to the pins. The pine boards make possible more ball action or spin. Range finders are the dark brown arrows built into the bed which serve as points of aim for "spot" bowlers.

Lane conditions vary considerably according to the manner in which they are finished and maintained. Some lanes which have just been oiled are called "holding lanes," meaning that they are fast and cut down on the amount of hook the ball will take; others may be slow or "running" and the hook will break too much and too soon. The experienced bowler, after rolling a practice ball or two, can determine or "read" the alley and can therefore make adjustments in his point of aim or in the technique of his delivery which will accommodate the ball to the type or condition of the lane.

Bowling pins usually are made of maple or laminated wood, weigh from three to three and one-half pounds each and are fifteen inches high. The specifications on size and weight of pins is rigidly controlled by the A.B.C. They must be unusually durable to withstand a 2,000 pound blow each time a bowling ball, traveling at an average speed of 15 miles per hour, makes a direct hit on a pin. A pin will last an average of 5,000 games.

Regulation balls have a circumference of twenty-seven inches, may weigh from 10 to 16 pounds and have two or three finger holes drilled to fit an individual's grip and type of delivery. See chapter 9 for details of a bowler's personal equipment including ball, shoes, bag, and clothing.

# Skills essential for everyone

# 2

Learning to bowl is largely a matter of developing the concept of toppling pins by rolling the ball at them smoothly and at the proper angle, instead of slamming the ball at them. To accomplish the "smooth roll" successfully, the learner must abandon his natural inclination to throw the ball down the alley with as much force as he can muster. This poses a problem to men who like speed. A ball thrown with uncontrolled speed is rarely synonymous with a strike ball. The weight of the ball and the distance to the pins are apt to make the beginner think that the faster he rolls the ball the sooner it will get to the pins without deviation, and that the more force it carries the more

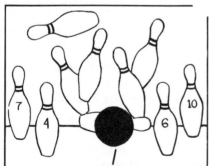

Pins "Fly"—Incorrect

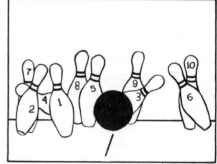

Pins "Topple"—Correct

Fig. 2.1

---

The suitability of a bowling ball depends on three principal factors. Can you name them? What difficulties related to each factor might be experienced in case the ball is not right for you?

---

pins will go down. While a certain amount of ball speed is necessary to knock the pins over, excessive speed causes the pins to fly up and off the alley instead of allowing the chain reaction of one pin hitting against another pin until all topple over. Of course, it is essential that the ball hit the pins at the correct spot for the chain reaction to produce a strike!

Before you ever lift a bowling ball to try the game, set your mind toward the objective of learning to "roll" a smooth, well-controlled ball.

## PREPARATION

Now that the challenge of rolling a smooth, well-controlled ball is firm and clear in your mind, there are a few preliminary steps to be taken before you step up to roll the ball.

First, dress appropriately to allow for freedom of movement. Bowling does not require a special costume although shirts and blouses should be loose around the arm and shoulders to assure an unhampered arm swing. Women bowlers should wear skirts or slacks which will allow for the knee bend and stretch in the sliding motion at delivery. Skirts should be neither too narrow nor too full, for either would restrict the delivery, and slacks should not be so long that they prevent a good sliding movement.

Bowling shoes are required in virtually all bowling establishments and can be rented as previously mentioned. Check out shoes, reserve a lane, and secure a score sheet at the checkout desk before going to a lane. Fees are paid upon the completion of your bowling when you return the score sheet and shoes to the desk.

Take time in selecting a ball from the rack. It is important to find one that is suitable in weight, span, and size of finger and thumb holes. House balls are usually arranged on the rack according to number and weight, and in addition may have the weight stamped on the ball. If you have never bowled before, probably all balls will seem heavy. In general, men should select a ball in the 14- to 16-pound range, and women should select one in the 10- to 12-pound range. The regulation maximum weight of a bowling ball is 16 pounds, and the minimum is 10 pounds. Lighter balls are made for juniors.

More important than the weight of the ball is the way it is fit to the hand. While "fit" is an individual matter, the method of determining the fit varies, depending on the type of grip chosen. There are three basic types of bowling grips—conventional, semifingertip, and fingertip. (see fig. 2.2). In the conventional or standard grip, the one which should be used in learning to bowl, the second and third fingers are inserted as far as the second joint. In the semifingertip grip the fingers are inserted midway between the first and second joint, and in the full fingertip the fingers are inserted only as far as the first joint.

The thumb hole should allow for the thumb to slide in and out freely. Test this by inserting the thumb all the way in the hole and turning it rapidly clockwise and counterclockwise. If this can be done with very little friction, then the thumb fit is proper. To determine the correct span or distance between the thumb hole and finger holes, insert the thumb as far as possible in the thumb hole and extend the hand and fingers over the contour of the ball so that the fingers stretch over the holes as shown in figure 2.3. The second joint of the middle finger should extend approximately ¼ inch beyond the inside edge of the finger hole. Do not forcibly stretch the hand in checking the span. Left-handed bowlers should use balls drilled correctly for them in order to have the correct location of the middle finger hole. It is set in about ¼ inch closer to the thumb hole than is the ring finger hole.

When you have found a ball that seems to fit comfortably, test it by gripping it and swinging it back and forth in a pendulum swing motion, then test one or two more balls and choose the one which feels best. The real test comes in rolling it, however, and you may wish to try out several different balls the first few times you bowl. Be particular, select the best available fit for you, until such time as you can purchase your own ball and have it drilled to fit your hand and grip.

A word of caution in picking up the ball from the ball return: right from the start, get the habit of picking up your ball from the return with both hands, to eliminate the possibility of finger injury or strain. Extend the hands on opposite sides of the ball away from any oncoming balls and lift the ball from the return as though there were no holes in it. Always face the alley as you pick up the ball. (see fig. 2.4).

Picking the ball up with the fingers in the holes is fatiguing and a strain on the fingers and arm, and besides, there is a possibility of dropping it on the approach, or worse yet, on your foot.

## BASIC SKILLS

Much of your success in bowling will depend on how well you master the preliminary actions necessary to the smooth, well-controlled delivery of the ball. As in any sport, learning and practicing the fundamental movement

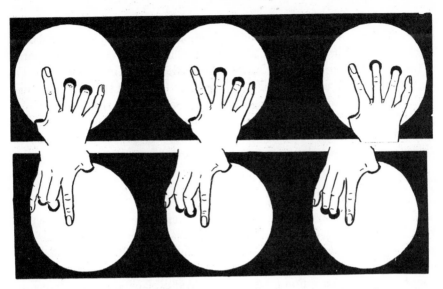

Conventional Grip      Semifingertip Grip      Fingertip Grip

Fig. 2.2   Three Types of Balls

Fig. 2.3   Checking the Span

Fig. 2.4   Correct Way to Lift Ball from Rack

patterns are necessary in order to achieve the best results—in this case to project a ball toward a given target as efficiently and accurately as possible. For the average person there is no shortcut to eventual optimum performance in an activity in which a ball or an object is involved, except through understanding of and dedicated practice in the fundamentals leading up to the actual projection of that ball or object. The preparatory actions, coordination of arm and leg patterns, the application of force, timing, and balance are as important in delivering a bowling ball as in putting the shot or serving a tennis ball. You can build on the required fundamental movements a certain style or minor unique action pattern better suited to your individual makeup, but the basic skills remain much the same for everyone.

NOTE: Keep in mind that all directions are given in terms of right-handed bowlers. Left-handers should transpose the phrasing of the directions to suit their needs.

### The Starting Position

The starting position can reflect individual preference as long as it is comfortable and relaxed. There are no hard and fast rules on how to address the pins except that you should face the target squarely, with your shoulders on an imaginary line at right angles to the target. Fix your eyes on the target or spot for which you are aiming. A more detailed explanation of spot bowling will appear in the following chapter. The position of your feet and the height at which the ball is held vary (see fig. 2.5). You may need to experiment with different stances and ball positions before you decide on one best suited to your timing and strength.

Determine where to stand in relation to distance from the foul line and distance from the right side of the approach. The proper distance for you to start from the foul line can be paced off by standing with your back to the alley bed at the foul line and pacing off 4½ normal walking steps toward the beginning of the approach. The half step allows for the slide as you roll the ball. Note the spot at which you arrive. The position toward center from

Fig. 2.5   Three Stances

the right side of the alley varies with the type of ball rolled. Until you have practiced enough to know what kind of ball (straight, hook, curve, or back-up) you will be rolling, it is safe to assume a position on the right side of the approach. The general inclination is to stand in the center and roll the ball down the middle of the alley bed at the center of the pins, but the strategic angle is from right to left for right-handed bowlers. Such an angle with slight individual variations allows for maximum toppling of pins. The angle and points of aim will be discussed in the following chapter.

Once you have experimented with several starting positions and have developed enough control and consistency to know how your ball is going to roll and what path it will take to the pins, then on each ball rolled you must check the starting position of your feet in order to improve your consistency and control. Check your heels or toes in relation to certain boards or the brown dots on the approach. It is essential that you *stand on the same boards each time you roll the first ball of a frame.* Depending upon the results of the first ball (that is, the position of the remaining pins) you may need to change your starting position for the second ball. These changes for the second ball will be taken up under spare-bowling techniques.

The ball should be held close to the body at chest or waist height and slightly to the right of the center of the body. Support the weight of the ball with both hands and insert the fingers and then the thumb in the holes in that order, remembering to grip a little more firmly with the fingers than with the thumb. The feet should be a few inches apart and on a line parallel with the target or spot, or the left foot may be a few inches ahead for a normal four-step approach. To make sure you get started on the correct foot, shift most of your weight to the left foot prior to taking the first step with your right. Bending slightly forward from the hips can be helpful in starting your forward approach with the push-away of the ball. An erect stance is also acceptable. The important point is to feel comfortable, to relax and to concentrate on the target.

To assist in relaxation as you assume the starting position, try taking a deep breath and exhaling slowly, then look to both your right and left to be sure there will be no distractions from other bowlers to upset your concentration as you make the approach to deliver the ball.

## The Approach—Four-step

The approach is the method of building up momentum for delivery of the ball by taking four walking steps forward in coordination with a pendulum-like swing of the right arm (see fig. 2.6).

Before concentrating on the mechanics of the approach, keep in mind that (1) speed is not the essential factor, (2) you are going to progress at

Fig. 2.6    Four-step Approach—Arm Swing and Step
Pattern

Ask an observer to check your competency in these important fundamentals: ball picked up correctly; starting position of feet consistent; shoulders
squared with target; ball moved before body moved.

a moderate pace rather than "charge" toward the foul line, and (3) you
will prepare to "roll" the ball instead of "throwing" it.

The four-step approach, while not the only one, is recommended and
used by at least ninety percent of the top bowlers. If you have tried to bowl
without instruction, you may have fallen into a three-step or even a five-step
pattern. Unless you have bowled for a number of years using one of these, or
a qualified instructor has allowed you to continue an odd step pattern because of your unusual ability or success with it, you should learn the four-
step approach. It is more rhythmic than the other approaches. If you are
using the three-step approach at present and are not too successful with it,
or if you have tried the four-step and get overly confused, try the five-step
which allows you more time to let the ball swing back. Both the three- and
the five-step approach start with the first step on the left foot, and it is
sometimes easier for three-steppers to change to a five- than to a four-step.
The three-step is the least desirable of the approaches.

Next, you must decide whether you are going to learn to roll a straight
ball, a hook ball, or a backup. Just as the four-step approach is recommended
by most expert bowlers, so is the hook delivery. The various types of deliveries are shown in figure 2.7.

Men bowlers and the majority of women bowlers should learn the hook
delivery at the very outset. Some instructors recommend that women in
particular learn to roll a straight ball first and then change over to a hook
after they have mastered the fundamentals and have adequate control. Unless a student has very small or weak hands and wrists, or the hook delivery
seems terribly awkward, he might as well start out with the technique and
delivery to be used eventually.

Now back to the approach. After you have assumed the proper and
relaxed starting position, hold the ball in both hands at a comfortable
height in front of you and slightly to the right of the midline of the body.
The left hand is under the ball supporting most of its weight. The right
hand grips the ball in the hook delivery position. The easiest way to describe
the hand position for delivering a hook is to drop your arms to your sides.
Now bend the right elbow so the lower arm swings up toward the right
shoulder without changing the hand position. This will result in the "handshake" or hook position of the thumb and fingers. This is the most natural
of the various hand positions or grips. If you concentrate on keeping the
wrist firm and holding this same hand position throughout the entire arm

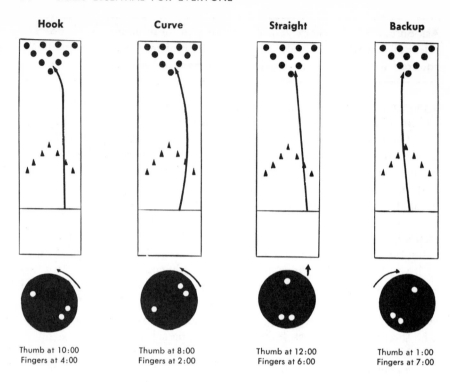

| Hook | Curve | Straight | Backup |
|------|-------|----------|--------|
| Thumb at 10:00<br>Fingers at 4:00 | Thumb at 8:00<br>Fingers at 2:00 | Thumb at 12:00<br>Fingers at 6:00 | Thumb at 1:00<br>Fingers at 7:00 |

Fig. 2.7    Four Types of Deliveries

swing pattern until after the ball is released, you will have no difficulty in rolling a hook.

To make sure you have the correct hand position prior to starting your approach, lift the ball from the rack as described earlier and turn the thumb and finger holes to their respective positions as shown in the first diagram of figure 2.7. The thumb hole should be at approximately "ten o'clock" and the finger holes at the "four o'clock" position. Insert the fingers first, then the thumb. Holding the ball comfortably in front and slightly to the right side of you as described earlier under "Starting Position," check to see that the wrist, forearm, and hand form a fairly straight line and that the elbows are close to the body. Watch to see that the wrist position remains firm and that the wrist does not collapse behind the ball.

From the stationary starting position, take a trial swing by pushing the ball forward, down, back, and forward again in a pendulum-like swing motion from the shoulder. Try this several times, feeling the ball swinging from the end of your arm. Do not attempt to lift or force the ball on the backswing. The arm should be straight and the hook grip maintained throughout the swing. There should be no rotation of the trunk, arm, or wrist during any part of this motion.

Once you are satisfied that the ball can swing smoothly and easily, and have made sure that the **V** formed by the thumb and first finger has remained on top of the ball during the forward swing, then the more complicated coordination can be attempted. This involves fitting the step pattern with the arm swing pattern. If the arm swing is natural, smooth, and continuous, then your attention can be devoted to the four steps taken in time with the complete arm swing.

If the first step of the approach is taken simultaneously with the push-away forward motion of the ball, the next three steps should coincide with the arm swing action in rhythmic sequence. This step is the most important one of the entire approach. As you push the ball out on a slightly downward angle at your right side, both hands supporting the ball, you will feel that the swing of the ball outward is causing your body to be pulled forward into taking the first short step on the right foot. If you first think of starting the ball and then move the right foot to make the short initial step almost instantaneously, you will have the correct timing. If you step and then move the ball forward, or even think about the step prior to moving the ball, you will probably be "out of time" and arrive at the foul line before you're ready to release the ball. Persons who hold the ball high in front of the chin or chest for the starting position should be particularly aware of the need to move the ball out just a fraction ahead of the first step. This is necessitated by the longer distance the ball must travel before it reaches the perpendicular in the arc, by which time the second step of the approach has been completed.

Inexperienced bowlers tend to move the body toward the foul line before moving the ball, and carry the ball along on the first step. Let the forward swing of the weighted ball "pull" you into the initial step. If timing is off at this point, you can be sure timing will be off at the foul line.

As the ball begins the downward arc let the left hand drop from the ball at approximately the same time you take the second step on the left foot. The second step should be slightly longer than the first. At this point the ball should be close and parallel with your right leg. If it is not in this position, you either have failed to remove your left hand from the ball soon enough or you may have released it too soon. In either case you will probably find that the ball is ahead of your slide or that you are ahead of the ball at the foul line.

As the ball swings on back and up toward the 180° or halfway point of the swinging arc, the third step is taken on the right foot. This step is

Can you maintain a firm wrist position as you practice swinging the ball back and forth? Can you swing the ball while walking without following a zigzag path?

again slightly longer than the previous step. The height of the backswing may vary. The normal apex of your backswing is usually about the same height in the swinging arc as your starting point on the push-away. Swing the ball back as far as you can comfortably control it, keeping your shoulders facing the target. Women in particular may not have the strength and therefore the control for a high backswing and should just let the ball swing naturally as far back as is comfortable and safe. Increasing the forward lean of the body from the hips on the second and third steps will result in a longer backswing. From this adjustment the arm muscles are assisted by more of the shoulder and back muscles. As a result the body is in a more mechanically efficient position, thus allowing the bowler with a weaker arm to obtain the additional ball speed that results from a longer backswing.

The third step is the most awkward for novice bowlers in that the right leg is forward and the right arm is back, a coordination which is in opposition to the more natural right-arm-back left-leg-forward pattern used in executing most sports skills. However, should you have difficulty with the third step, walk the pattern out slowly and practice it several times without the ball. Remember, on the backswing the arm should be in a "pendulum

Fig. 2.8  First Step—Push-away

Fig. 2.9  Second Step

motion," *swinging straight back* close to the right side. *Keep the shoulders and trunk facing the target.* There is a possibility of a crooked backswing or overswinging if you allow the trunk to rotate to the right or drop your shoulder.

The fourth step is more of a slide than a step and is longer than the three previous steps. Execute the slide on the left foot simultaneously with the forward swing of the ball. The fourth step will vary in length with different bowlers, and should take the same amount of time as does the forward swing of the ball. Remember that the first three steps were involved with the first half of the arm swing pattern and only *one* slide step is taken for the second half of the arm swing prior to the release of the ball. The length of slide then actually depends on the speed with which the arm and ball swing forward. Don't be misled by this statement and attempt to rush the forward swing or forcefully "throw" the ball down the alley. You will not have the feeling of rushing to the foul line if you were "in time" on your previous steps, especially the first one. Still maintain the important thought of "rolling" the ball off the fingers and down the alley. In sliding on the fourth step, slide with most of the weight on the ball of the foot. Bend the left knee and shift most of your body weight onto the sliding foot. This insures the "braking" action necessary to check the forward momentum of the body. The left foot should stop the sliding motion two to six inches from the line to keep you from "fouling." Make sure that your left foot is pointing straight ahead, and that your shoulders are facing the target.

Fig. 2.10   Third Step                Fig. 2.11   Fourth Step

Can you identify the type of ball delivery shown in the diagram? What would the delivery have been called if the ball had curved to the right?

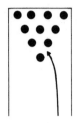

As the ball swings forward to a point beyond the perpendicular, or opposite and beyond the sliding foot, release it by letting it roll easily off the thumb and fingers in that order. The ball should contact the alley bed in front of the foul line. Have the feeling that you are lifting the ball just over the line. To do this successfully, of course, the body and ball should reach the foul line at exactly the same time, and your arm should reach out toward the target and follow on through in an upward arc, elbow bent slightly as if reaching toward the ceiling. At the release or "explosion point," the right hand should still maintain its "shaking hands" position—thumb at ten o'clock and fingers at four o'clock. The standard hook delivery will automatically evolve if you concentrate on the foregoing techniques—the correct hand position, thumb slipping out of the ball first, and entire hand following straight through in an upward arc at the end of the swing. If proper hand position is maintained at release and the ball does not hook, concentrate on firmer finger pressure inside the finger holes as you swing the ball forward. You must feel the ball roll off the fingers last and the fingers pull upward at release to give what is known as a "lift" to the delivery of the ball. Note the bent elbow position of the arm on the follow-through in figure 2.6. It is not necessary to force a hook by twisting the trunk, swinging the arm across in front of the body or turning the hand over.

Observe in figure 2.12 the balanced follow-through position of the bowler at the foul line. The follow-through is as important to the bowler as it is to the baseball pitcher, the golfer, the javelin thrower, and so many others. Any athlete projecting a ball or an object toward a target will attempt to guide that object in a direct line by maintaining contact with the object as long as possible in order to achieve the desired angle of flight. A strong and well-balanced follow-through will also insure optimum speed of the ball. Novice bowlers who have insufficient strength tend to slow down on the forward arm swing motion even before the release of the ball, with the

Fig. 2.12    Fourth Step and Release (Courtesy of National Bowling Council)

result that the ball rolls very slowly and is apt to deviate more on its way to the pins.

Study figure 2.12 and review these most important "check points" of the fourth step:

1.  Weight on the left foot
2.  Left knee bent
3.  Left foot a few inches from the foul line and pointing toward your target
4.  Right leg extended behind body for balance
5.  Left arm extended to the side to aid in balance
6.  Shoulders facing the target
7.  Body leaning forward at the line so that foot, knee, and shoulders form a vertical line
8.  Eyes focusing on the target or spot

Most expert bowlers will "pose" or hold their delivery position until well after the ball has been released to insure proper balance and position during the ball release. This is a "must" for control, consistency, and high scores. All learners should set a goal for themselves and exaggerate the follow-through by attempting to pose for three counts after release—until the ball is over a certain spot on the alley, or until the ball hits the pins. Maintaining a well-balanced delivery position after releasing a heavy ball is probably the most difficult of all the bowling techniques. Concentrate on perfecting it with every ball you roll.

Most of your success in bowling will depend on how you perform *behind* the foul line. When the ball isn't rolling to suit you, go back and

Have you incorporated all the following key points in your approach and delivery?

1.   Pushing the ball away on first step
2.   Walking straight toward the foul line
3.   Concentrating on a spot
4.   Sliding on your left foot
5.   Maintaining your balance
6.   Delivering the ball out over foul line
7.   Lifting your hand on the follow-through

check each of the fundamentals—the stance, the approach, the delivery, and the follow-through; better still, have your instructor or an expert bowler check them for you.

### Straight Ball Delivery

For students who have difficulty controlling the hook, or for students who lack strength in the hands and wrists, the straight ball may prove more successful.

The fundamentals for delivering a straight ball (see figure 2.7) are the same as for the hook. The differences are in the grip of the ball at the start and hand position at release.

Hold the ball in the starting position in front of the body in exactly the same manner as you would for the hook, but rotate the ball so that the location of the thumb hole is at the twelve o'clock position. The finger holes are at approximately six o'clock. This grip allows more of the hand to be under the ball, providing some additional support as the ball is swung. The same "thumb-on-top" grip is also in effect as the ball is released at the foul line; however, the fingers slide out of the holes before the thumb. This is the reverse of the hook release.

The straight ball will have no spin; it should be released near the right gutter and roll on a diagonal line from right to left into the 1-3 pocket. The term "straight" means the absence of a hook or curve but the ball should not be rolled down the middle of the alley.

# Better players
# master these techniques

# 3

It may be difficult for you to determine just when you should classify yourself as a "better player." Some beginners endowed with great natural ability may reach this category in relatively few lessons or practices while others may take one or two years to master the fundamentals. In addition to the amount of natural ability you possess are the factors of desire, motivation, and your ultimate objective in learning the game. Do you want to learn just enough to "have fun with the gang" or do you really want to perfect each of the basic skills, learn the fine points of the game, and become an accomplished bowler? If your intent is toward the latter objective then you should allow plenty of time for instruction and buckle down to a good deal of practice. You should feel satisfied with each stage of your performance, and particularly with what goes on behind the foul line, before you tackle the fine points of the game. On the other hand, bowling is not such a complicated sport to learn that the person with average skill can't "have fun" and knock down some pins after only a few lessons and a little practice. He may never get out of the "120" class in this "shortcut" program but a couple of strikes and spares per line can give him the enjoyment, recreation, and exercise he wants or needs.

In either case, or for a person falling in the middle category between the two, the bowler should first be able to move his body and the ball "in time" up to the foul line, release the ball smoothly, and maintain balanced control of the body behind the foul line. Once the basic movement patterns have been learned and have become automatic, ball control, accuracy, and consistency can be improved. This does not imply that you must be an experienced bowler before working on accuracy and consistency in the path the ball takes to reach the target. These are also very important in learning the game. A "better bowler" does not need to think about what he is going to do with his body in delivering the ball. He can concentrate on improving his aim, being more scientific in picking up spares, putting more "stuff" or spin on the ball, or studying more of the strategy of competitive bowling. Aiming and picking up spares are important parts of learning the game, but these techniques are not considered fundamental. A student could, by instinct or by trial and error, arrive at some method of aiming or picking up the remaining pins, but to become an average or accomplished bowler, he should learn a more scientific and effective method.

## METHODS OF AIMING

There are three common methods of aiming the ball to get maximum pin fall. They are pin bowling, spot bowling, and a combination of the two— line bowling. Each will be described, and you may wish to experiment with all three before choosing one. However, if you wish to save some time and rely on statistics and recommendations of the experts, select the spot method. Almost all of today's top bowlers use this method. It is recommended for beginning bowlers mainly because the target (spot) is only 16 feet away as compared to one 60 feet away if the pins are used as a point of aim. It has also been found to be a more accurate and scientific method of picking up spares, correcting faults, or making allowances for variations in lane conditions.

The line method is the next most common method used. In it the bowler pictures an imaginary line painted on the lane over which his ball will travel. He also makes use of several checkpoints along this line and concentrates on these as the ball progresses down the lane.

The least desirable point of aim is the pins themselves, unsatisfactory because of their distance from the delivery point. Individuals who are extremely farsighted may have better results with this method, but it is not generally recommended.

Whatever the system you choose, remember that bowling is based on the use of angles. For the proper chain reaction which will result in a strike, the ball contacts certain pins, then other pins hit against each other and are toppled. The standard hook ball must "drive" into the 1-3 pocket, breaking from right to left, and make a solid hit on the 5 pin. You should select whichever system of aiming will enable you to accomplish the strike most consistently.

## Pin Bowling

By definition, this is the term applied for aiming directly at the pins. The pins, in general, cover a rather large area. Since the objective is to hit the 1-3 pocket, most pin bowlers will use the dark space between the one and three pins as the specific point of aim. They should also select a starting position on the right side of the approach and walk in the direction of the 1-3 pocket to insure the ball's coming into the pocket on the right-to-left angle. Many novice bowlers start out pin bowling because this is all they see or know. They erroneously bowl from the middle of the alley and aim at the headpin. Another disadvantage to pin bowling is the inclination for the bowler to follow through incorrectly or pull up too soon. The focus should be at the base of the pins to aid him in staying down on the follow-through.

## Spot Bowling

In this method, which is strongly recommended, you, the bowler, focus your eyes on a designated spot or board in the alley about 16 feet from the foul line. You do not look at the pins until the ball has crossed over your spot or target. This idea may seem strange at first because you are trying to hit the 1-3 pocket without looking at it, but it works. You also plan to arrive at the foul line so that your

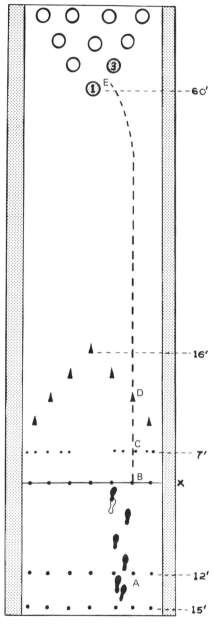

Fig. 3.1.    Checkpoints  for  Spot Bowling

right shoulder is in line with the spot. This enables your arm to follow straight through toward the spot so that the ball, when released, will roll over this target. Actually a good spot bowler uses several other spots as check points to make sure on his approach that he stays in line with the "spot" out on the alley. The spots indicated in figure 3.1 are used for the strike ball.

This diagram shows the checkpoints used by a bowler with an average hook ball. Once you have a consistent hook ball you will need to experiment with your checkpoints. If your ball hooks more than this you should pick a spot one or two boards to the right of the second arrow ("D"); if it hooks less, then try one or two boards left of arrow. You can also move your starting position one or two boards right or left to give you more or less angle going into the pins.

*The Starting Position*    Before you make your four-step approach, look down at your feet and see if they are placed in exactly the same position for every first ball you bowl. The first set of dots at the rear of the alley is 15 feet back of the foul line and is used by most men and by tall women with a long stride. The second set of dots is 12 feet from the foul line and should be used by persons with a shorter stride. Be specific and see that either the toes or heel of your right or left foot are in a certain location relative to one of the dots. Also make sure that your starting position is to the right of center so your hook will break from right to left into the pocket.

Notice that the foot position at "A" is slightly left of the second checkpoint, "B." This allows for the right shoulder to be over "B" at the release point.

*The Release or Footwork Checkpoint*    Your release point ("B") is actually beyond the foul line but your hand and the ball should swing over the second dot or in close proximity to it. The "B" checkpoint also helps you to walk a straight path to the foul line during your four-step approach. Take a quick glance at the second dot as you go into your approach because you obviously cannot look down to check it as you release the ball. If you have a tendency to "drift" or walk to the left in the approach, have someone sit directly behind you and watch to see how far left of the second dot you deliver the ball. An even better method of correcting a crooked approach is to check your left foot position in relation to the dots at the foul line. If you are walking straight up to the line your left foot should stop just short of approximately the third dot from the right and your left foot should point straight ahead. Of course you must maintain your balance at the foul line in order to be able to check the left foot position at "B."

How is your concentration? After delivering a ball, can you tell by how many boards, if any, you missed your spot? If you hit the headpin but failed to make a strike, can you account for what happened?

*Angle Spots*    These are 7 feet beyond the foul line and may be used to check the angle your ball is taking. Some nearsighted bowlers prefer to use one of these as "the spot" or point of aim instead of one of the usual "D" spots.

*Point of Aim*    This is the all important "spot" in the spot bowling technique. Actually it is not a spot but a brown arrow or dart built into the alley. There are seven of these arrows (called "the range finders") to help you find your range on both strikes and spares. You must keep your eyes glued on your spot as you approach, release, and follow-through. Watch the center of the ball roll over the spot. There is a great temptation to look up too soon to see if you get your strike.

One of the chief advantages of the spot method is that if you're really watching the ball in relation to a "D" spot, you can compensate your aim. Suppose you have rolled three balls in a row which have hit the headpin and left you with splits. You then have a choice of shifting your point of aim one or two boards to the right of your original spot, or of moving your starting position slightly to the left, using your same spot. Either move will have the same corrective effect. Do not be too hasty in changing your spot. Wait until a repeated error develops.

*The 1-3 Pocket, or Strike Pocket*    If all four previous spots have "checked out," you should end up with a 1-3 pocket hit. This may happen and yet for some reason you don't get a strike. There is a point of accuracy even within the pocket and, depending upon which pins are left standing, you usually can analyze what went wrong. It takes a while to determine which niche in the pocket is right for your ball. In general, if you are leaving splits or corner pins, you're in the pocket but the ball is hitting too squarely on the headpin. If you leave the 5 or center pins you are usually too light on the headpin.

Should you miss "E" completely, but hit all other checkpoints, your trouble could be in the ball release. Your approach and follow-through may have been straight to the spot but you may have turned your wrist too much to the right or the left, or may have released the fingers before releasing the thumb, causing the ball to go straight instead of hook. Additional tips for improvement can be found in chapter 4.

### Line Bowling

The line bowling system is a combination of spot and pin bowling. The bowler who line bowls usually imagines a black line painted on the lane which runs from the range finders or a spot on the alley, to the pins. This line approximates the path his ball should take. This system is often more desirable than pin bowling for the hook bowler because he "sees" the curved line hooking into the 1-3 pocket.

## PICKING UP SPARES

Your ability to pick up spares (to knock down the pins remaining after bowling your first ball) can make up the difference between your becoming a low- or a high-average bowler. Too often beginning bowlers are so engrossed with the idea of getting strikes that when they miss on the first ball, they hurry the process of rolling the second ball and throw it carelessly at the remaining pins so that they can more quickly get at the next full set of pins. Calculate for a minute the possibility of your rolling a 180 or 190 game without even making a strike. You have merely to be accurate in converting a one- or two-pin leave in each frame into a spare.

Of course the object of bowling is to knock down as many pins as you can on the first ball. If your first ball is too far off the mark you are going to leave pins standing that will be difficult for you to knock down for a spare. But there are, comparatively speaking, very few leaves that cannot be spilled from the alley by a well-placed second ball. With the proper know-how and practice on various spare angles, the average bowler can learn to clear the ally at least 90 percent of the time. The other 10 percent of the time may find him faced with "impossible" splits. The good bowler knows that he must calculate, rolling his second ball very carefully to make sure that the one or two "key" pins struck by the ball are hit in such a manner that they will knock any other pins off the alley. How is this done?

First of all, keep the delivery style on your second ball consistent with that of your first ball. Make only those few adjustments that are absolutely necessary; they should be mainly in the starting position or in the point of aim. The type of ball you roll should remain the same, that is, if you roll a hook, stick with the hook on each ball. Some spares may appear rather impossible to get with a hook but it can be done. Do not switch to a straight ball on your second ball, not even on difficult leaves. If all else is forgotten, plan on hitting the pin closest to you to get your spare.

Likewise your method of aiming should remain the same on both balls. If you spot bowled the first ball then do so on the second. Many beginners who learn to spot bowl on the first ball decide to look at the pins on the second ball because it is simpler and less time-consuming than figuring out a new spot or adjusting the starting position so many boards right or left. Actually the adjustments are not that difficult to determine once the concept of the three basic spare angles is understood; they are the middle spare (5), left-side spare (7), and the right-side spare (10).

As a general plan, in converting left- and right-side spares, angle the ball across the lane at the remaining pins. This gives you maximum lane surface over which to roll the ball. Observe in the diagram that the main adjustments occur in the position of the feet at the beginning of the approach, the dot over which you release the ball at the foul line, and your spot for aiming. With this system of picking up spares, the second and third arrows or somewhere in between the two are the only targets needed. You may need to deviate one or two boards, depending on the lane conditions and the extent of your hook.

Take time to figure out the best angle for converting a particular spare, contemplate which pins the ball will get and which pin(s) will topple other pins. In your early days of learning watch other bowlers attempting to pick up spares and notice how the ball deflects when it hits the pins. It angles quite

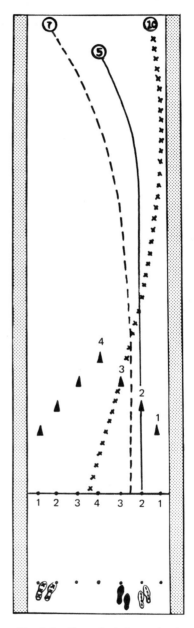

Fig. 3.2    Three Basic Spare Angles

sharply right or left depending on the approach angle, the number of pins it is contacting and whether it hits the right or left side of the pins. It does not continue on a direct path straight through the pins. Note the right and left deflections in figure 3.3.

Occasionally you may observe a bowler, even an expert, who will roll a straight ball at the right-side spares or who moves his starting position and his spot a few boards left for left-side spares. This is done especially if the 2-pin is involved in order to narrow the angle and prevent a "cherry pick" or "chop" in certain situations. This is called "covering" your spare.

Here are a few examples of some rather common leaves with suggestions as to best ways of converting them into spares. One general rule, if all else is forgotten: plan on hitting the pin closest to you to get your spare.

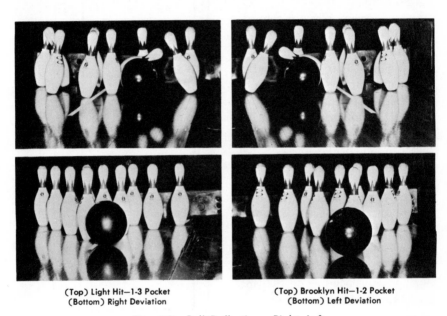

(Top) Light Hit—1-3 Pocket
(Bottom) Right Deviation

(Top) Brooklyn Hit—1-2 Pocket
(Bottom) Left Deviation

Fig. 3.3　Ball Deflections—Right, Left

### Middle Spares—Strike Ball Position

Figure 3.4(a). The 5 or "kingpin" is usually left up because of a light hit on the headpin.

Try your strike ball again, making sure you concentrate on your spot. A single pin in the center of the lane is one of the easiest spares to get. You have a 23-inch target—combined width of two balls (9-inch width) and the pin (4¾-inch width).

Figure 3.4(b). This leave is called a "sleeper" and is a difficult one to spare without "cherrying." To prevent this, you must hit the 2 pin quite solidly. For a right-handed hook bowler, this can be done by shooting a

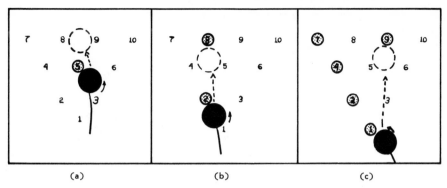

Fig. 3.4    Middle Spares

strike ball if you move your feet and your spot about two boards left, giving you less angle and decreasing your chances of picking off the 2 only. The ball hits the 2, the 2 kicks off to the left and the ball goes back on a deflection slightly right and gets the 8.

Figure 3.4(c). This is a deceptive leave for the inexperienced bowler. On first glance it appears that a headpin or 1-2 pocket hit down the middle would be the answer. With these hits you undoubtedly would leave up the 9. Here is where ball deflection is of prime consideration. If the ball hits left of the headpin, it will deflect left after the hit—the 1, 2, 4, & 7 will go down but the 9 will remain. A strike ball hitting the right side of the 1 will cause a chain reaction of the 1, 2, 4, & 7, and the ball will deflect right and go back to take out the 9.

### Left-Side Spares

These include leaves on the left side of the lane with the ball being delivered from the right side.

Figure 3.5(a). Begin the approach about five boards or one dot to the right of your usual starting position to give you the widest angle and the most alley surface. Face toward the 7 pin and walk in that direction on your approach. Release the ball between the first and second dot and spot the second "D" arrow or one or two boards to the left of it, depending upon the extent of your hook. Do not "loaf" or ease up on the delivery, because the ball must carry the hook to the last row of pins. The tendency is to get too much angle and roll into the gutter before reaching the pin. Remember there is more space on the right of the 7 pin than on the left.

Figure 3.5(b). This spare results from a very thin hit on the right of the headpin. It is easy to "pick" either the 4 or 5 pin so you must come into the 2-5 pocket strong enough to cause the 2 to take out the 4 and the ball to deflect slightly right to go back and get the 5 pin.

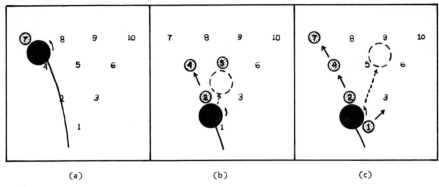

Fig. 3.5 Left-Side Spares

Even if you pull your ball left you may still hit the 2-4 pocket and the 2 pin will get the 5 pin.

Assume your strike ball position and bowl between the second and third arrows for a Brooklyn hit.

Figure 3.5(c). Here is a case of the ball not hooking and so missing the headpin. The safest play is a 1-2 pocket ball because the ball contacting the 2 will cause the chain reaction of the 2 hitting the 4 and the 4 hitting the 7.

Use your far right starting position from the first dot and aim for the second arrow. The 1-2 pocket is not as far left as the 7 pin, therefore your right to left angle need not be as great.

This spare can be converted with a well-aimed strike ball, but this is risky. If your strike ball is a little wide you miss all the pins, whereas if you pull the 1-2 pocket ball you may get 2 or 3 pins anyway.

### Right-Side Spares

These include "leaves" on the right side of the lane and the delivery should be made from the left side. Right-side spares are usually more difficult for the right-hander to convert. The occasions when he must bowl from the left side are not as frequent, and his ball hooks away from right to left instead of hooking into the pins as is the case in the left-side spares.

Figure 3.6(a). This is a very difficult single pin to pick up because it is sitting just 2½ inches from the gutter.

Start from the extreme left, feet near the far left dot. Face the pin and walk toward it. Release the ball between the third and middle dots from the left and aim at the third arrow from the right. Be sure you follow through strongly. If you give up too soon you will pull the ball left and miss.

**Have you taken time to practice any of the five most common spare leaves? (a) ten; (b) seven; (c) five; (d) one, two, four; (e) six, ten.**

Beginners tend to get too much angle and go into to the right gutter, so try aiming one board left of the third arrow if you have this difficulty.

Figure 3.6(b). Again start in the far left position and walk toward the pins. You want the ball to hit the right half of the 3 pin so you won't need quite as sharp an angle as for the 10 pin alone. Aim for a point between the third and middle arrow from the right.

Hitting the right half of the 3 will send the 6 pin against the 10.

Figure 3.6(c). This spare is more of a right center spare than a far right spare like the 3-6-10. It requires slightly less angle and the ball hooking into the left center of the headpin. This angle sets up the chain reaction and the ball deflects back to knock down the 8 pin. Start left of center and aim for the center arrow or one or two boards to the right of the center, depending on the amount of hook on the ball.

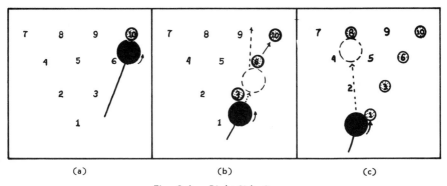

(a)          (b)          (c)

Fig. 3.6.   Right-Side Spares

### Splits

A split is a "leave" of two or more pins with the headpin down and a gap of at least one pin between any other two pins. A split occurs when your first ball hits too "heavy" or "high" on the headpin.

Figure 3.7(a). "Fit Ins" are so called because the ball must be accurately placed between the two pins to convert the spare. Actually the space between the two pins is only about two inches less than the ball width. Therefore your angle must be accurate for the ball to hit both pins.

In each case which is the key pin that must be struck first if the spare is to be picked up? 1, 2, 4, 7, 9; 2, 8; 2, 4, 5; 3, 6, 10; 6, 7, 10?

Bowl this from a starting position about one dot left of center, spotting the third arrow. This is a right center spare and will not require as much angle as a 10-pin spare.

Figure 3.7(b). The 7 pin is a row behind the 6 pin; consequently the ball must hit the 6 pin not only on the right side to slide it over but must hit toward the front right side to slide it over at the proper angle. Bowl from the left side and spot for the 10-pin position so the ball will hit thinly on the 6 pin.

Figure 3.7(c). It is practically impossible to get all four pins unless one pin flys back into the kickbacks and rebounds onto the alley to take out the remaining pin in the split. Try for two or even three pins. From your experience decide whether the 4-7-10 or 6-7-10 is easier and pretend you have just three pins remaining. The ball will contact the two corner pins, the 6-10 and the 6 will slide over and take out the 7. Aim for either the 10-pin or 7-pin hit so the 6 or 4 will be hit thin and slide over.

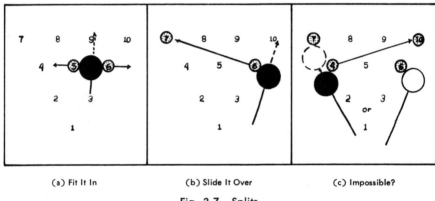

(a) Fit It In        (b) Slide It Over        (c) Impossible?

Fig. 3.7    Splits

## Taps

A tap is the chief lament of the better bowler because it seems to be a solid pocket hit but for some strange reason one pin is left standing. For the right-hander the most common tap is the 10 pin, others are the 8, 9, 7, and 4. Other single pin leaves are not usually the result of solid pocket hits. Taps are an unlucky part of the game and must be taken in stride. They are not due to the ball action but to one pin flying around another pin instead of taking it out. There is no remedy except positive thinking!

## INFORMATION FOR ADVANCED STUDENTS OF THE GAME

### Types of Ball Roll

For the average "once a week or less" bowler, the standard hook or straight ball is adequate. Most experts will agree that unless you are doing a great deal of competitive bowling two or three nights a week plus several hours practice a week, you should not attempt a "fancy" delivery that you can't control. However if your ball lacks action or "stuff" so that you're getting very few strikes you may want to experiment with or get some instruction in learning to roll a different type of ball. You might also try out a fingertip or semifingertip ball to aid you in more lift at release. If you do attempt a change in style or type of ball roll, you must be prepared to face a drop in average temporarily while you erase the old habit patterns and build new ones.

*Semiroller or Three-Quarter Roller*    The most popular of the hook balls is the semiroller and the one that has been discussed throughout this book. It is probably the strongest of the hook balls but it is the timing of the release with the lift which determines the effectiveness of the hook. The semiroller rolls on a track (the surface of the ball which contacts the lane) anywhere from one-half to three-quarters of the ball's circumference. The ball should roll somewhere below the thumb hole to about two inches outside the thumb hole. The narrower the track on your ball the more consistent you are in rolling it. A ball rolling over the thumb hole sounds lopsided and loses "stuff" every time. This is a result of turning the wrist so that the thumb is down at release.

To effect a semiroller all you need to do in addition to your regular hook ball grip is to lift the wrist upward and inward so the wrist is in a slightly cocked or flexed position at release. The fingers apply the lift (from the four o'clock position) moving upward and following the outward contour of the ball to about the two o'clock position at the time of release.

*Full Roller*    The full roller is delivered much like the straight ball except for the position of the thumb and fingers at release. Instead of the fingers letting go from behind the ball (five o'clock position) on the straight ball delivery, they release from the side of the ball at about the three o'clock position. The lift is straight up with no broken or cocked wrist positon as in the semiroller. It rolls on its full axis with the track not over an inch in width and appearing between the thumb and finger holes.

*Semispinner*    For bowlers who feel a natural inclination to roll or turn the wrist at release the semispinner may be an effective type of ball. The regular hook ball grip is used but at the explosion point in the release the wrist turns counterclockwise so that the fingers are at about two o'clock and the thumb at eight. There is also some finger lift at release. The track for the semispinner is wider and cone-shaped.

*Full Spinner*   This is a weak type of hook and is not recommended, particularly on fast lanes. It is released with little or no finger lift and with the wrist turning counterclockwise from a thumb-on-top position to a finger-on-top position. This puts terrific spin on the ball but it is difficult to control under certain unfavorable lane conditions.

*Backup*   This is another type of delivery that is not recommended because of the unnatural hand position at release and the troubles with control. It is being described only for those (particularly women with weak wrists and hands) who start to develop a backup so that they will recognize it immediately and do something about it. A back up may develop when a person learning to roll a straight ball attempts to put more speed on the ball. She may twist the wrist clockwise so the thumb is at the one o'clock position at release and comes out of the ball after the fingers. The ball fades to the right, breaking away from the 1-3 pocket, so the backup bowler usually aims for the 1-2 pocket and bowls from the left of center on the approach. This is the least desirable type of ball roll and angle.

### Ball Action

If you closely examine a hook or curve ball rolling down the lane you will notice that the average ball skids about fifteen feet (to your spot), then rolls the next twenty feet and finally turns for the last twenty feet. At the beginning of the final twenty feet or turn, the spin motion is overcoming the forward motion of the ball. For this reason the ultra fast ball is ineffective. It skids farther, rolls less and hooks very slightly, thus giving little opportunity for the pins to mix.

   With a curve which is a much slower delivery (but more difficult to control), the ball does not skid so much and the roll turns into a curve sooner taking more spin at the finish. If your curve quits on you, it is because it has started to hook too soon and you need to throw the ball out more on the alley.

### Lane Conditions

No two bowling lanes are the same. Each pine board may have a different amount of pitch and it is the pitch that slows up the ball. A reddish colored board will have more pitch in it than a yellowish colored board, and it will "take" to the spin of the ball, thus producing a more decided hook. This is called a "running lane." An increased friction on the lane caused by dust on the ball or on the lanes, or lanes used late in the day after the oil has dried, will all lead to slower lane conditions and thus an exaggerated hook. A "holding or stiff lane" is one which is faster and holds down the action of the hook. The lessened curve is caused by a lack of friction which reduces the sideward spin of the ball. A highly polished lane or a lane which has just been oiled will be fast and the ball will not hook as much. With the lacquer being used on the lanes, it is very difficult to see where the balls have worn a track. There is a very thin oil dressing (only two ounces on an entire bed) so only an expert can detect the track. The only way you can tell what the alley will do to your ball is to bowl on it.

In order to adjust to alley conditions you must move to the right or left of your usual starting angle, depending on how the alley affects your usual delivery. If your ball is not "finishing"—missing the headpin on the right, then move slightly to your right to get a sharper angle. The reverse is true if you are pulling the ball into the 1-2 pocket. Move your starting position to the left. Watch to see that you do not move so far to the left that your body is to the left of the headpin, for this is a difficult angle from which to make strikes because of the deflection of the ball.

### Bowling Strategy

As in other sports, the strategy of the game depends on the situation. If you are bowling an important team match where each pin down is vital, you may use a different strategy than you would in an informal game with friends. In the latter situation where your performance affects only yourself, you may take many more chances in converting difficult splits than you would if your team were depending on you.

One of the first things you can do is to study the tournament temperament and how the various individuals on the opposing team react to pressure. Some bowlers thrive on competition; others get to a point where they cannot relax. Some are great front runners and are terrific as long as they are in the lead, but as soon as someone catches up with them, they fall apart. Others get better under pressure and have to get behind to throw a relaxed ball. These are the strong finishers. Study the psychological strategy first; some later decisions may depend on how well you know your opponents.

Another important part of bowling strategy is the making of decisions on how to bowl against splits. If you happen to draw a split (or even a large

The ball has a diameter of 8½ inches and there is less than 8 inches between any two adjacent pins. How many spare leaves can you list that
should be rolled by "fitting the ball in"?

cluster of pins) after a strike, be certain to "count" down as many pins as
possible because each extra pin down counts as two in the scoring. Always
be very careful after a strike and do your best to strike again or at least hit
the pocket and get a big count.

In most situations after a split occurs, play it safe and attempt to get
one pin of two or two of three. If you are the last man and the game or
match depends on your conversion, then of course you must try it. Many a
game is won or lost by a pin or two. Never try to convert the "railroads"
(7-10, 4-6, 7-9, etc.) by sliding one pin into another. Your chances are very
remote and you will often miss both pins by trying to hit one lightly on the
side. Again, if you need to "go for broke" in this situation your chances are
better if you roll the ball into one pin solidly and slam it into the cushion and
hope it will fly back into the other pin.

Understand the importance of the "ninth frame" strategy. Try your
best to strike in the ninth so you can lay a foundation and develop a relaxed
feeling for your tenth frame. Remember, with two extra balls it is possible
to "turkey out" in the tenth. One last bit of advice, yet one of the keys for
team success, is that you be "strategic" with yourself. Relax, concentrate,
take "the bitter with the better" and work toward being a dependable, consistent bowler. You are much more valuable to your team with these attri-
butes than you are as an erratic, temperamental individual who bowls 220
one game and 120 the next.

# Progress
## can be speeded up

# 4

By now you should have an understanding of what abilities and achievements are necessary for becoming an accomplished bowler. The methods you choose for progressing rapidly toward them are likewise important. Obviously the best method is a program of instruction and guided practice with a qualified bowling instructor. The next best thing would be a few lessons on the fundamentals of delivery, some additional reading, study, and observation of what the experts recommend, and then a great deal of self-directed practice. A periodic check by your original instructor will save you time and effort in the undoing of the wrong habit patterns which can develop so quickly.

## CONDITIONING, WARM-UPS, AND PRACTICE TECHNIQUES

Although bowling is not as rigorous as many other sports, the swinging of a 12-16 pound weight on the end of your arm for any period of time can be fatiguing to the unconditioned. Before starting out on a "training program" for becoming an accomplished bowler, make sure you have adequate strength in your right hand and arm and a sturdy left leg. The following exercises are recommended primarily for women bowlers who may lack initial strength.

### Improving Grip Strength

1. Squeeze a small rubber ball (handball size) in the palm of your right hand. Hold the hand in the regular hook position, relax the thumb and

squeeze the ball with the second and third fingers about twenty times twice a day.

2. Practice swinging a bowling ball back and forth. While you're waiting your turn to bowl, move to the back of the seats or to an uncongested walkway and swing the ball continuously back and forth until your arm is fatigued. Use your regular hook grip and retain this grip throughout the swing process. Try to increase the number of swings you do at a time, each day you do the exercise.

### Strengthening the Left Leg

Walking, and going up and down stairs keeps your legs in good enough condition for the amount of bowling done by the average bowler. For beginning bowlers, however, merely balancing on the left foot, knee bent, left arm extended sideward, right arm extended forward in the normal follow-through position is not only a good exercise for the thigh muscles but will help improve your balance.

### Developing the Proper Arm swing

Your arm swing is important. The arm should be kept close to the body. Develop the same swing forward, back, and forward again. Practice your swing with a towel folded under your arm. If it drops, you arm is not swinging in the correct path or arc.

### Coordinating the Approach and the Delivery

When you don't have time to go to the lanes, practice on the sidewalk with a rubber ball or a softball. Measure your approach and use chalk to mark the foul line and the arrows. Take your four-step approach with slide and see how smoothly you can release the ball and how many times it will cross the proper arrow.

## SPECIFIC AIDS FOR COMMON FAULTS

Probably the two most common errors made by all inexperienced bowlers are improper timing of the steps and arm swing on the approach, and poor balance and follow-through at the foul line.

By using the one simple remedy of slowing down the approach you may avoid one or more of the following errors: (1) forcing the ball, (2) bouncing it, (3) dropping it, (4) drifting, (5) fouling, slipping, or sticking at the foul line, or (6) delivering a ball that fails to come into the pocket but stays to the right of the pocket. The easiest way to slow down the approach is to shorten the first step (and possibly the second and third), shorten the push-away and start it simultaneously with the first step, and most important of all, think of rolling the ball smoothly as you progress toward the foul line.

If you have attempted to slow down your approach but your balance and follow-through are still poor, check the following remedies: (1) On the fourth step slide with the weight on the left foot, just as you would if you were sliding on ice; (2) bend the left knee as you slide and shift most of the body weight to the left foot, lowering the heel as you slide to act as a brake in stopping forward momentum; (3) extend your left arm out to the side to counterbalance the release of the weight (ball) from your right side; (4) keep your left foot pointed straight and your shoulders facing your target or spot; and (5) lean forward and reach strongly straight out toward your spot after the ball has been released.

## OTHER COMMON FAULTS AND THEIR REMEDIES (See fig. 4.1)

### Improper Arm Swing Pattern

1.  *Too high a backswing* leads to loss of control and perhaps too much speed for a good working ball.

    Remedy: Do not allow your trunk to rotate to the right ("side-wheeling") on the backswing. Keep your shoulders facing the target and allow the ball to swing back to a comfortable height . . . straight back in line with the target.

2.  *Too low a backswing,* common among women bowlers, usually results in insufficient speed on the ball. This plus the lighter ball used by women bowlers makes it difficult to get many strikes.

    Remedy: The first thing to do is to strengthen the grip if you are swinging short for fear of dropping the ball. Move the ball to a higher starting position under the chin, thus allowing more time and a longer swinging arc to build up momentum for a longer backswing. Practice swinging the ball back naturally as far as it will go and after it has reached the apex of the arc, let gravity and the weight of the ball furnish the forward swing power.

3.  *Crooked backswing* causes the arm to swing out too far from the body on the backswing or in too far behind the body; the result is a diagonal

Dropping the Ball

Poor Balance

Compensation

Sidewheeling

Drifting to the Left

Drifting to the Right

Fig. 4.1    Common Faults

forward swing in the opposite direction and the ball will go too far right or left of the mark.

Remedy: Swing the ball straight back close to the right side toward an imaginary target behind you in line with your right shoulder. Keep your shoulders and trunk facing your target. Then swing the ball straight forward toward your mark out on the alley.

## Overturning or Turning the Ball Too Soon

This results in trying to put too much "stuff" on it so that you twist or jerk the ball at release.

Remedy: Let the ball do the work by letting your thumb and fingers slide out of the ball easily and smoothly. Make the release a flowing motion. Wait until the ball has passed your left foot on the forward swing before you break or lift the wrist. The weight of the ball may cause the wrist to turn slightly, but do not force a turn.

## Missing Your Point of Aim

If your angle is bad or lane conditions are such that you are consistently missing your spot to the same side, try changing your starting position to allow for more or less angle, as the case may be.

1. *Consistently left* of your spot means too much angle or ball released too soon.

   Remedy: Move your starting position only a few boards left. Keep your same point of aim.
2. *Consistently right* of your spot means not enough angle or ball released too late.

   Remedy: Move your starting position a few boards to your right, keeping your original point of aim.

## HINTS FOR LEARNING AND PRACTICE

In addition to good instruction and reading about some of the fine points of the game, your learning can be enhanced by watching the experts. Watch their various styles of delivery on television or go to your nearest bowling establishment the night the scratch leagues are bowling, find out which are the bowlers with the highest averages, and observe them closely. Sit directly behind them and concentrate on their straight line approach and follow-

**Can you pick off the 10 pin and then the 7 pin from a full rack without knocking down any other pins?**

through, then move to a position where you have a side view of their timing of the steps and arm swing and their body position at the foul line. Concentrate on the bowlers themselves in action and not the pins going down. Also observe their methods for picking up spares and splits. As soon as the first ball is bowled and if pins remain, quickly analyze your procedure for the second ball and see if the bowler does what you would have done in the same situation. This mental practice can be used when bowling with friends or watching others bowl on adjacent lanes. How would you pick up those spares if your were doing it?

One of the best aids in learning a new activity is the motion picture. Study films of the experts, or have movies taken of your performance and compare it with those of the experts.

Practicing a great deal at the bowling alley may run into some expense and it may become difficult to discipline yourself to practice instead of bowling games. Typically, watching the pins fall down and scoring begin to take most of your attention and you neglect concentrating on fundamentals. Bowling without pins or "shadow bowling" is practically a must for proper learning of the fundamentals of the approach and delivery. Go to the lanes when they are not busy and pay your money to just roll the ball for an entire line. Do this as many times as is necessary to develop a smooth, rhythmical, mechanical delivery. After this has been accomplished, bowl many lines without keeping score. Re-rack the pins each time until you consistently hit your pocket.

You may want to practice with a friend and let him work on spares (that you leave) while you concentrate on your first ball. To discipline yourself make drawings of the lane with the arrows and a set up. Chart the path of your ball as it crosses the arrow you have chosen as yours, note the ball's hook, and circle the pins that are left standing. Then write the reasons for your error (fig. 4.2a). In order to diagram the path of your ball you must keep your eye on the arrows; you will be able to discern if you have a consistent hook pattern; writing down your reasons for error will insure that you are concentrating on just what you are doing. You can use the same type of chart when you are working on spares. First, determine your strategy and draw the approach and path the ball should take; then after you have bowled, use a dotted line to indicate the path your ball actually took (fig. 4.2b). Hopefully, the two lines will coincide.

## Practice Chart

Diagram the path of *your* ball as it crosses the arrow and hooks. List reasons for
your error.

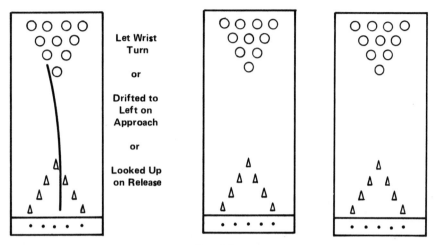

Fig. 4.2a

Diagram the path the ball should take. Use a dotted line to indicate path of *your*
ball. List reasons for your error.

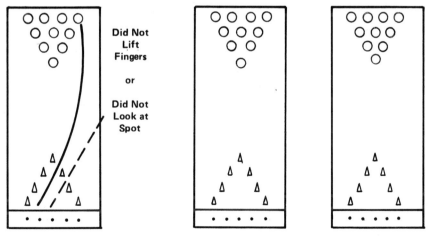

Fig. 4.2b

Fig. 4.2   Learning and Practice Charts

---

Prepare a practice sheet with the pins diagrammed for each frame as shown. Draw a line through each pin knocked down by the first ball and circle pins picked up by the second ball. After four or more lines, can you discover any consistency in first ball or second ball errors? If so, what are appropriate corrections?

---

Another practice essential is to spend time working on your right-side and left-side spares. With the pins up, try a line of bowling attempting to pick off just the 7 pin or just the 10 pin. The automatic pin machines make it difficult to practice spare bowling but you can practice your various spare angles to see if you're hitting your spot.

Dedicate yourself to a few hours practice by yourself so you can concentrate your full time on the task at hand. Once you start keeping score, make notes to yourself on the score sheet, particularly in regard to your spot. You may discover some objective evidence of first or second ball inconsistencies. If possible, try to practice some every day or several times a week rather than long hours over the weekend. Consistency is developed faster by regular practice than by intermittent sessions.

# Understanding the challenge and the mechanics of bowling

# 5

This may be your first bowling venture, yet you have already rolled a perfect frame (made a strike) and picked up a difficult—if not impossible—spare. And therein lies one of the basic reasons for the popularity of bowling—the ease and simplicity with which it can be performed. The technique of the game is one exercise (combination of movements) repeated over and over again in an attempt to make the pattern consistent. To develop this consistency to the point of machinelike precision and thus record a perfect game of three hundred is almost impossible. Herein lies the fascinating challenge of the game. Yet the possibility of continuing to improve your score is almost unlimited.

If you are serious about your game and want to become a student of bowling, then you need to question why particular techniques are recommended or if there is one best method to follow. A knowledge of the mechanical principles involved in bowling should help you understand why certain errors occur and the reasons specific movement patterns are suggested.

Successful bowling consists of applying to the ball sufficient force, in an effective direction, that (it) will knock down all ten pins. A degree of strength is necessary in order to obtain the required force, but the control of direction is the more important of the two factors. Due to the length of the lane, a very slight deviation in the path of the ball when crossing the arrow (range finder) can result in a change of the ball's point of contact by as much as a foot from its target point after it has traveled the remaining forty-six feet to the pins.

## THE BEND AND THE SLIDE AT THE FOUL LINE

You have already discovered the particular point of aim that is most successful for you. The problem that remains, then, is to roll the ball over that spot
with more consistency. The bent knees and subsequent lowering of the body
enables you to get closer to the arrow, thereby improving accuracy by short-
ening the distance to the target. Reaching out toward the arrow on the
release shortens this distance even more. Also, it is easier to balance when
one's center of gravity is low and over a wide base, and a smooth release is
easier when the bowler is not working to maintain balance.

Releasing the ball with the hand close to the lane as opposed to bowling from an upright position also gives you a smoother roll. Since the ball
is traveling a short distance in the air it will initially skid, i.e., slide forward
without rotation as it touches the lane. The ball then travels with linear
motion (moves forward at a uniform rate of speed) and rotary motion
(spin).

If the ball is lofted, the linear and rotary motion are adversely affected.
A lofted ball skids more and lands farther out on the lane; therefore, it
doesn't have enough distance to hook before reaching the pins.

**Developing a Hook Pattern**

Grip

Release

Follow Straight Through With Lift

Fig. 5.1    Four Essentials of Hook Ball Delivery (Courtesy of
the National Bowling Council)

---

If the lane is said to be fast, would you be apt to change your spot to the right or left of your usual mark?

---

Rolling a hook is accomplished by applying force off center. The thumb comes out of the ball before the fingers, and since the fingers are at four o'clock, on the right side of the ball, the off-center force is applied from the right; result—the right to left hook pattern. The lifting action of the fingers following the forward arm swing causes the ball to roll forward; then it hooks. Initially, the forward momentum of the ball is greater than the speed of the spin so the ball travels in a straight path for a distance of twenty to twenty-five feet before curving to the left. The spinning action does not affect the ball until its speed is reduced by the friction of the lane.

A number of factors can cause deviations in the hook pattern. The ball must slide off the thumb first so the final force is applied by the fingers which must be on the right side of the ball; failure to lift on the follow-through will lessen the spin and decrease the angle of the hook. A ball thrown with too much speed will skid farther and have less distance to hook before reaching the pins, and a slow ball will start its hooking pattern too soon and be left of center before it reaches the pins.

Lane conditions also affect the amount of hook, so the bowler must apply the basic principles governing a hook delivery and take into consideration the running or holding action of the lanes as outlined on page 35.

## PIN ACTION

A degree of strength (force) is necessary to prevent the slow ball mentioned above, and to get the optimum pin action when the ball enters the pocket. The headpin contacted on its right side by the ball will take out the number two pin and it in turn (or in combination with the one) will take out the four. Four will take out seven; or one, two, and four may combine to topple seven. At the same time, the three pin hit by the ball will take out the six, which will, in turn, take care of number ten. After the ball moves through the pocket it will contact the five which takes out eight; then the ball continues through to contact the nine pin. On a perfect hit the ball contacts only four pins, and these four pins are responsible for the remaining six.

If the ball is thrown with too much force the pins with which it comes in contact are swept off the lane vertically, i.e., they leave the lane in a virtually upright position and do not take out the pins behind. A ball rolling too slowly also has poor pin action. Such a ball has little spin (from lack of force or insufficient hook) and is more easily deflected by the pins. Consequently, the path of the ball is altered.

---

**Do you know several mechanical principles you can employ to give you a faster rolling ball?**

---

With any pin contact the ball is deflected somewhat, but the ball is much heavier than the pins and because it is moving, the force exerted by the ball against the pin is much greater than the force of the pin against the ball (see fig. 3.3, p. 28). From this, it can be concluded that the heavier the ball the less its path will be altered by contact with the pins. Therefore, it is best to bowl with as heavy a ball as can be easily controlled.

### EFFICIENT MOVEMENT USED TO GAIN STRENGTH

A bowler would be more accurate if he stood at the foul line taking time to aim his ball at the arrow, but this would result in a slow-rolling ball with little pin action. An arm swing back, then forward would give a little more momentum to the ball but the sheer weight of the ball makes this a difficult movement.

The walking approach combined with the arm swing gives additional force since the momentum of the body is transferred to the ball. The ball takes on the motion of the body just as a rider takes on the motion of a vehicle in which he is riding. If you step off the moving vehicle (car or merry-go-round), you will continue to move. The ball acquires the same motion as the hand and will continue to move when released with the same speed until it contacts the lane and then other forces alter its speed.

Even though accelerating the approach would increase the speed of the ball it would make braking extremely difficult, see page 17); therefore the bowler determines the speed of his approach by the control needed to stop on balance just short of the foul line.

In addition to using the momentum built up during the approach, ball speed (force) can be increased by lengthening the arm swing (see page 16). If the ball is held higher, at chin level instead of at chest level, and/or the push-away is increased, gravity will aid in the attainment of a longer arm swing. If the swing is lengthened then the stride must also be lengthened, because it is vital to have the arm swing coordinated with the approach to take advantage of the momentum mentioned above.

The arm should swing naturally at the side letting gravity act on the ball to bring it down and back. Leaning forward will increase the height of the backswing, and this lean is also useful in balancing the ball at the top of the backswing. The approach should be in a straight line since any sideward movement detracts from the forward momentum and interferes with accuracy.

## SUMMARY

It becomes apparent that the bowler cannot overemphasize one aspect of the game. The man who hurls the ball with great speed often leaves himself with a difficult split, and so does the woman who rolls a puff ball that goes right into the strike pocket. Bowling should combine strength, grace, and timing. Strive to incorporate all three, apply the basic mechanical principles of efficient movement, then develop your own style.

A bowler gains satisfaction in being able to perform an efficient movement pattern, and enjoys a sense of accomplishment in controlling the body; in addition, there is the bonus of pleasure in seeing the pins fall because of a well-directed hit. Bowling's attraction is the ease of movement inherent in the game; and, paradoxically, its simplicity is its greatest challenge.

# The language and lore of bowling

# 6

*Bowl* is thought to be derived from the Saxon "bolla" and the Danish "bolle," both meaning, in the literal sense, bubble. The word later referred to any round or spherical object. Some authorities trace the word to the Latin *bulla* or round ball, and others prefer the French derivation *boule*, meaning ball.

Throwing, pitching, or rolling objects at targets has for centuries fulfilled an innate urge in man, and the earliest records of such activity used as a game were discovered by an English Egyptologist, Sir Flinders Petrie. While examining the contents of an Egyptian child's grave, the burial date placed at 5200 B.C., he discovered implements and objects for playing a game very similar to our tenpins of today.

In other studies by Dr. Malcolm Rogers, curator of the San Diego Museum, an ancient bowling game as performed by the Polynesians was found in which small elliptical balls and round, flat discs of stone, about 4 inches in diameter were used. The game was called Ula Maika and consisted of bowling or rolling the stones a distance of 60 feet, the length of our hardwood lanes today.

Bowling's place of origin in Europe appears to have been in what is now Northern Italy, where as early as 50 B.C. the Helvetii played "Boccie," a game similar to the modern Italian bowling.

These ancient forms of bowling more closely resembled lawn bowling. Bowling at pins actually originated as a religious ceremony in the cloisters of cathedrals in Germany as early as the third or fourth centuries A.D. It was then the custom for the canons to test the faith of their parishioners by having them place their pins at one end of the cloister and from the opposite end throw a ball at the pins which represented the "Heide" or heathen. If a hit was scored this meant the parishioner was leading a pure and clean life and would be able to slay the heathen; if he were unsuccessful at hitting the pins it meant that in order to improve his aim he would need to be more faithful in attendance at church services. Those who were successful were called "keglers" and were honored and toasted at a dinner given at the conclusion of the tests.

The game ceased to be a religious endeavor and developed into a sport when the canons became intrigued and began "kegling" with their cathedral students. The game changed to include as many pins as there were keglers.

The first indoor bowling lanes are believed to have originated in England where, because of bad weather conditions, bowling on the open green was difficult. During the Middle Ages, to insure year around activity, the wealthy enthusiasts of the game constructed bowling annexes to their residences.

On the continent, bowling or ninepins soon became a universal pastime. In Germany, Martin Luther was an enthusiastic bowler and built a bowling lane for his family. The French had a game called Carreau which was played

Fig. 6.1  Early Egyptians Bowling (Courtesy of American
Bowling Congress)

What is the name of the hit shown in the diagram? What causes the ball to roll in this manner?

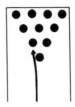

long before the reign of Charlemagne. The Dutch Pins version resembled skittles but with taller and narrower pins, especially the middle pin which was higher than the rest and called the kingpin. Curling, another adaptation of the ancient game of bowls, was introduced into Scotland by the Flemish in the sixteenth century. Bowling on ice became very popular in countries with severe winters.

In America, the early Dutch settlers brought the game of ninepins with them to Manhattan Island in 1626. Three citizens leased a plot which had been used for a parade ground or marketplace; this area was located at what is now the foot of Broadway in New York City. They enclosed it for a bowling green and the little park still bears its original name of Peppercorn.

Washington Irving in his "Rip Van Winkle" (1819) made one of the earliest references to pin bowling when he mentioned the thunder of the ball colliding with pins. The early game probably reached the height of popularity in the 1840s in New York where bowling lanes were found on nearly every block on Broadway and in various parts of the Bowery. Most of the matches were rigged, and this led to the abolition of bowling in New York, Connecticut, and Massachusetts by a law in 1841 which declared it a gambling game. By 1850 gamblers and swindlers had complete control of the game of ninepins.

The game of ninepins, which had the pins set in a diamond formation, had been condemned by the Puritans two hundred years earlier because men were devoting time to playing that could have been better spent in work. However, neither condemnation nor legislation could abolish the enthusiasm for the game. Thus ninepins at that time had to be played on the sly. Many a bowler sat in the stocks or in prison for his defiance of the law. An ingenious hero, noting that the long-standing law prohibited "bowling at nine pins," added a tenth pin and a triangle formation which not only circumvented the law but improved the game, and its growth began. By 1875 the game became well enough established for the formation of a "National Bowling Association" to revise the rules and standardize the equipment. Although great credit is due this early association, it failed to survive and the American Amateur Bowling Union followed in 1890. It too disintegrated due to its limitations, giving way to the American Bowling Congress, whose objective was to help promote and elevate the game. As a result of insight, purposeful planning, and principles this organization is today the largest sports organization in the world. The Women's International Bowling Congress was established in 1916, and the American Junior Bowling Congress, governing the instructions and competition of bowling for boys and girls, developed soon afterwards.

Bowling establishments are no longer thought of with ill respect and as an unwholesome atmosphere for women and children. With the construction of large bowling centers containing 100 lanes or more, together with lounges, dining rooms, and even nurseries, bowling has lost its unsavory "pool hall" association and has become one of the largest participating sports and one of the most popular forms of family recreation in the United States.

## BOWLER'S LINGO

Almost every sport has a language uniquely its own and bowling has what is probably one of the most colorful vocabularies of all. If you should bowl in various parts of the United States, you may need to learn a new terminology. Bowlers in Los Angeles and Chicago call a 1-2 pocket hit for right-handers a "Brooklyn," whereas the Brooklynites call it a "Jersey." Most of the terminology listed here is widely used but space is left for you to insert other lingo peculiar to your locale.

Remember that to master all aspects of bowling you should "talk" a good game as well as demonstrate it.

### Terms Relating to the Ball

*Backup.* Ball that curves to the right for a right-handed bowler.
*Bridge.* Distance between finger holes on the ball.
*Brooklyn.* Ball hitting to the left of the headpin (1-2 pocket) for right-handed bowlers.
*Creeper.* A very slow ball.
*Crossover.* Same as "Brooklyn."
*Curve.* A ball that has a wide sweeping arc.
*Dead Ball.* A poorly rolled ball which deflects off course.
*Flat Apple* or *Flat Ball.* Same as "dead ball."

Flat Apple

*Gutter Ball.* A poorly rolled ball which goes off the lane into the gutter before reaching the pins.

*Hook.* A ball that breaks to the left as it nears the pins for a right-handed bowler.

*Loft.* Throwing the ball too far out on the lane beyond the foul line.

*Pitch.* The angle at which the finger holes are bored in the ball.

*Span.* Distance between thumb and finger holes.

*Working Ball.* A very effective hook ball with much pin action or spin.

Others:

........................................................................................................................

........................................................................................................................

## Terms Relating to the Bowler

*A.B.C.* American Bowling Congress.

*Anchor.* A person bowling in last position on a team, usually the one with the highest average.

*Choke.* To tense under pressure.

*Foul.* Touching or going beyond the foul line as the ball is delivered.

*Kegler.* Another name for bowler (antiquated term).

*Scratch Bowler.* A bowler who has no handicap—topnotch.

*W.I.B.C.* Women's International Bowling Congress.

Others:

........................................................................................................................

........................................................................................................................

## General Terms Relating to the Lanes

*Alley.* Another name for lane.

*Approach.* The area on which the bowler takes his steps prior to delivering the ball at the foul line.

*Channel.* A modern term for the gutter.

*Foul Line.* The line that separates the approach from the lane.

*Graveyard.* The lane or lanes which are toughest for a bowler to score on.

*Gutter.* Either side of alley bed which catches misdirected balls, or errant pins.

*Kick Backs.* The division or side boards at the pit end of the lane.
*Return.* The track on which the ball rolls back from the pit to the ball rack.
*Spot.* A certain place on the lane at which the bowler aims. Range finder.

### Lane Conditions

*Holding.* A fast lane which cuts down on the amount of hook.
*Rough, Tough,* or *Mean.* Lanes which are difficult to score on.
*Running.* A slow lane which allows more hook.
*Soft.* Lanes which are easy to score on.
*Stiff.* Same as fast or holding lane.

Others:

........................................................................................................................

........................................................................................................................

### Terms Relating to the Pins

*Baby Split.* The 2-7 or 3-10 splits.
*Bedposts.* The 7-10 split.
*Big Four.* The 4-6-7-10 split. Also known as "double pinochle."
*Bucket.* The 2-4-5-8 leave.
*Cherry.* Picking off the front pin of a spare and leaving other pins standing;
    also referred to as a chop.
*Headpin.* The number one pin.
*Kingpin.* The number five pin.
*Leave.* The pins remaining after the first ball is rolled in a frame.
*Pocket.* The space between the 1-3 pins for a right-handed bowler; space
    between the 1-2 pins for left-handed bowler.
*Railroad.* Synonym for split.
*Sleeper.* A pin hidden directly behind another pin.
*Split.* Two or more pins standing with intermediate pins (in front and in
    between) knocked down.
*Tap.* Leaving a 10, 4, or 7 pin on what appeared to be a strike ball.
*Washout.* The 1-2-4-10 leave for a right-hander; the 1-3-6-7 leave for a left-
    hander.

Others:

........................................................................................................................

........................................................................................................................

### Terms Relating to Scoring

*Blind.* Score given a team for an absent member.

*Blow.* An error. Failure to spare (except following a split).

*Double.* Two strikes in succession.

*Dutchman.* A 200 game consisting of alternating strikes and spares.

*Frame.* The box on the score sheet in which the score is registered; one-tenth of a game (aside from game-end bonuses).

*Handicap.* A method of scoring which enables individuals or teams with different averages to compete against one another.

*Line.* A game of ten frames.

*Mark.* Getting a strike or spare.

*Open Frame.* A frame without a strike or spare.

*Scratch.* Using actual scores without handicaps.

*Spare.* All pins knocked down on two balls.

*Steal.* To get more pins than you shoot for.

*Strike.* All pins knocked down on the first ball.

*Strike Out.* Three successive strikes in the tenth frame, or striking to finish the game.

*Turkey.* Three strikes in a row.

# Scoring and rules of the game

# 7

A game or line of bowling for an individual consists of ten frames. The bowler has ten attempts, rolling one or two balls, to knock down all ten pins in each frame. The game score is the total number of pins knocked down in the ten frames.

The symbols for scoring are marked in each frame as follows:

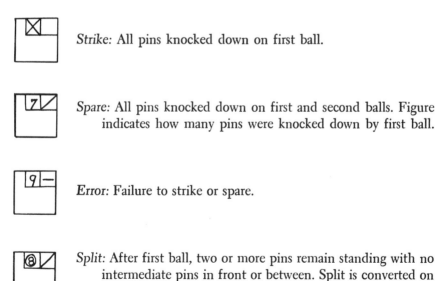

*Strike:* All pins knocked down on first ball.

*Spare:* All pins knocked down on first and second balls. Figure indicates how many pins were knocked down by first ball.

*Error:* Failure to strike or spare.

*Split:* After first ball, two or more pins remain standing with no intermediate pins in front or between. Split is converted on second ball.

**Fill in the score in each frame for the line of bowling shown in the diagram.**

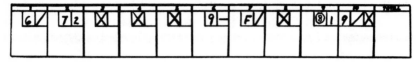

  *Foul:* When a part of the bowler's person goes beyond the foul line. When a player fouls, no score is allowed on that ball.

Actually scoring a game of bowling is quite simple if you follow four basic procedures:

1. *No strike or spare.* Merely add the total pins knocked down on first and second ball and score as follows: Scoring is accumulative.

2. *Strike.* Ten plus a bonus consisting of the number of pins knocked down on the next two balls rolled.

3. *Spare.* Ten plus a bonus of the pins knocked down on the first ball of the next frame.

4. *Tenth Frame.* If a spare occurs in the tenth frame, the bowler is entitled to roll one more ball. If a strike occurs in the tenth frame, the bowler is entitled to two additional balls to finish the game.

## HELPFUL HINTS

A combination of strike-spare or spare-strike in successive frames is always 20. Strike = 10 + next two balls. Spare = 10 + first ball in next frame.

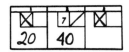

A "double" or two strikes in a row is always twenty something (2-?) depending on the number of pins knocked down on the first ball rolled after the double, i.e., 10 + 10 + 8.

A triple or "turkey" scores 30 and is the highest figure which can be recorded or added on in any one frame, i.e., 10 + 10 + 10.

NOTE: This is how a perfect game of 300 can be scored (10 frames of 30 each).

The general playing rules for bowling are few and much less complicated than for most sports competition. The A.B.C. and W.I.B.C. are responsible for the rules and their interpretation. There are some technical rules involving the proper functioning of leagues which, because of lack of space, will not be listed here. They can be obtained by writing the A.B.C. or W.I.B.C. These are the important general rules.

## OFFICIAL GAME[1]

The bowling of ten complete frames on a pair of lanes on which the game was started shall constitute an official game, unless equipment failure delays the normal progress of the game and in such cases the game or series may be finished on another pair of lanes.

---

1. From the official rule book of the American Bowling Congress. Reprinted with permission.

The members of a team shall successively, and in regular order, bowl one frame on one lane, and for the next frame alternate and use the other lane, so alternating each frame until the game is completed.

In league play, the first game of a series shall be started on the lane on which a team is scheduled. Succeeding games shall be started on the lane on which a team has finished the preceding game.

### Fouls

A foul is committed with no pinfall being credited to the player, although the ball counts as a ball rolled, when a part of the bowler's person encroaches upon or goes beyond the foul line and touches any part of the lane equipment or building during or after executing a legal delivery. A ball is in play and a foul may be called after legal delivery has been made and until the same or another player is on the approach in position to make a succeeding delivery.

Leagues must have a foul judge or an electric foul detecting device in operation. The captains of the opposing teams are responsible for the calling of fouls in the event of mechanical failure of the foul detecting device, and a foul judge is not available.

If a player deliberately fouls to benefit by the calling of a foul, he shall be immediately disqualified from further participation in the series then in play and his place is taken by another player. The deliberate foul shall not be allowed.

A player who willfully throws his ball into the gutter shall be immediately removed from the game and series and his place may be taken by another player.

If no substitute is available, his team shall be credited only with the pins knocked down up to the time the player was disqualified plus one-tenth of his absentee score for each of the remaining frames in the game.

A foul ball shall be recorded as a ball bowled by the player, but any pins bowled down when a foul is committed shall not count. When a player fouls upon delivering the first ball of a frame, all pins knocked down must be respotted, and only those pins knocked down by the second ball may be counted. If all pins are bowled down with the second ball after fouling with the first, it shall be scored as a spare. A player who fouls when delivering the second ball of a frame shall be credited with only those pins knocked down on the first ball, provided no foul was committed on the first ball.

### Pinfall

*Legal*—Every ball delivered by the player shall count, unless declared a dead ball. Pins must then be respotted after the cause for declaring such dead ball has been removed:

1. Pins which are knocked down by another pin or pins rebounding in play from the side partition or rear cushion are counted as pins down.
2. It is the player's responsibility to determine if the pin setup is correct. He shall insist that any pins incorrectly set be respotted before delivering his ball.

**There are a few instances in which a pin knocked down cannot be scored legally. Do you know what these are?**

3.   Pins which are knocked down by a fair ball, and remain lying on the lane or in the gutters are termed dead wood, counted as pins down, and must be removed before the next ball is bowled.

*Illegal*—When any of the following incidents occur, the ball counts as a ball rolled, but pins knocked down shall not count:

1.   When pins are knocked down or displaced by a ball which leaves the lane before reaching the pins.
2.   When a ball rebounds from the rear cushion.
3.   When pins come in contact with the body, arms or legs of a pinsetter and rebound.
4.   A standing pin which falls upon removing dead wood or which is knocked down by a human pinsetter or touched by mechanical pinsetting equipment shall not count and must be replaced on the pin spot where it originally stood before delivery of the ball.
5.   Pins which are bowled off the lane, rebound and remain standing on the lane must be counted as pins standing.

### Dead Ball

A ball shall be declared dead if any of the following occur, in which case such ball shall not count. The pins must be respotted after the cause for declaring such dead ball has been removed and the player shall be required to rebowl:

1.   If, after the player delivers his ball and attention is immediately called to the fact that one or more pins were missing from the setup.
2.   When a player bowls on the wrong lane or out of turn.
3.   When a player is interfered with by a pinsetter, another bowler, spectator, or moving object as the ball is being delivered and before delivery is completed, the player must then and there accept the resulting pinfall or demand that pins be respotted.
4.   When any pins at which the bowler is bowling are moved or knocked down in any manner, as the player delivers the ball and before it reaches the pins.
5.   When a player's ball comes in contact with any foreign obstacle.

### Replacement of Pins

Should a pin be broken or otherwise badly damaged during the game, it shall be replaced at once by another as nearly uniform in weight and condition as possible with the set in use.

A broken pin does not change the score made by a bowler.

# Unwritten laws

# 8

There is more than score that reflects how much a player knows about the game and how desirable he may be as a team member or bowling companion. He must behave like a true sportsman and show the common courtesies and respect to other bowlers on his team and on adjoining lanes that he wishes shown to him. Bowling etiquette is merely a demonstration of everyday politeness and of allowing other bowlers to concentrate fully on the task at hand.

A bowling center, because of its size, numbers of people bowling, and type of equipment, presents a difficult atmosphere in which to concentrate; therefore, respect the wishes of the individual on the lane and remain quiet until he has finished his turn. Then congratulate him and show enthusiasm for a job well done; pep and chatter at the proper time do wonders for the morale of the team. Know the personalities and temperaments of the people with whom you bowl. Some can take a lot of kidding or razzing while others may be insecure and need encouragement.

## PRIORITY

Respect the bowler who is on the approach ready to make his delivery. Remain on the bench until it is your turn to bowl, then move promptly.

Wait until a bowler on the adjoining lane has delivered his ball before you step up to take your ball off the rack.

In general, give priority to the bowler on your right if he is ready to start his delivery at the same time you are. However, the bowler who has his

Fig. 8.1   Timely Tips on Bowling Etiquette. Distracting fellow bowler by lifting ball off rack at the wrong time.

spare to shoot has the right of way over the one who is rolling his first ball unless he motions you to go ahead. He may wish to contemplate his spare for a little longer.

There is an unwritten rule that if a bowler has a split left standing he will immediately take his second ball, so that the pins are cleared away. A bowler on an adjoining lane may not wish to see an awkward split staring him in the face when he is about to roll.

Between balls step back on to the floor behind the approach. The adjacent bowler may thus proceed without interference.

### CONFINE "BODY-ENGLISH" TO YOUR OWN ALLEY

Keep your balance and control at all times. Limit your actions to the width of your own lane.

### OBSERVE THE FOUL LINE

This goes for practice games as well as for league play. Sliding carelessly beyond the foul line may develop into a habit that is difficult to break. If you foul frequently, try taking a shorter first step or move your starting position farther back.

### SHOW CONSIDERATION FOR THE LANES AND EQUIPMENT

Replace house balls in their proper places on the rack after you have completed your bowling.

Check the number of your ball and use the same ball on the first and second attempts in a frame. Do not roll a different ball for your second roll.

Certain courtesies toward bowlers in adjacent alleys are expected. Have you these unwritten rules in mind?

The machines are timed to operate during the return of your original ball to the rack.

Refrain from blaming the equipment. The fault is probably yours and you should correct it.

Watch lofting the ball on your delivery. Use chalk or dry your hands if the ball is sticking. Lofting also may be due to poor timing on the release.

Show consideration for keeping the approaches clean by confining eating and drinking to the bench area and by making sure your bowling shoes are clean. Change to bowling shoes before stepping onto the approaches.

Be sure the pin machine rack is up before you roll!

## SHOW GOOD SPORTSMANSHIP AT ALL TIMES

Control your temper and your language. Constant complaints about bad luck or poor alley conditions are in bad taste, and you may become very unpopular as a bowling companion or teammate.

Refrain from giving advice unless you are asked for it. A bowler who is bowling badly may become more confused than ever. The best advice is "take your time."

Watch your bragging. It is best to let your scores speak for you.

Accept defeat gracefully and congratulate your opponent or opponents for their good bowling.

## KNOW THE PINS BY THEIR NUMBERS

This helps to speed up play, particularly if pins have been moved or knocked down accidently by the machines (or pin boy) and need to be respotted.

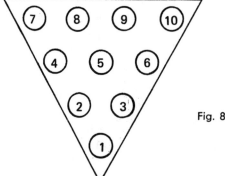

Fig. 8.2   Learn Number of Each Pin

# Facts for enthusiasts

# 9

Once you have learned the fundamentals of bowling and have become enthusiastic about improving your scores and becoming a competent bowler, proper fitting personal equipment becomes a must. Rented or "house" balls and shoes are adequate for learning the game, and up to that point at which you have ceased experimenting with different weights, spans, and types of balls. However, as in any sport, the caliber and fit of your equipment may help or hinder your performance. By all odds, you will bowl much more consistently with your own ball and shoes.

A custom-fitted ball is also much less likely to cause blisters, swollen knuckles, and perhaps even pulled muscles.

## SELECTION AND PURCHASE OF A BALL

### Weight

The selection of a "house" ball according to weight was discussed in chapter 2. Before you purchase a ball, try out several house balls of different weights. Keep in mind that lighter balls which fit poorly may seem to weigh more than a heavier custom-fitted ball. In the learning stages it is best to start with a lighter ball until proper timing and control are perfected and then change to a heavier ball which, all things being equal, tends to get more pins down and stays "on line" better. Very few women bowlers can handle a 16 pound ball without dropping it or becoming excessively tired so a 12 or 14 pound ball is usually recommended. Some men of slight build or older men may do better with a load of 14 or 15 pounds.

### Fitting

In having a ball drilled to fit your grip, be sure you deal with a reputable bowling manufacturer or custom driller who knows his business. There are some measuring gadgets on the market that are not reliable. Remember that a poorly fitted 14 pound ball can feel heavier than a well fitted 16 pound ball.

Most dealers who sell balls employ an expert driller and the purchase of a ball will entitle you to custom fitting and drilling at no cost.

The question of the number of finger holes is debatable for men but most women should stick to the conventional three-fingered ball. The two-fingered ball and the "finger tip" ball require more strength, control, and endurance. Many of the top performers today are using the "finger tip" ball but they usually bowl ten to twenty-five games a day and have developed excellent control and stamina. Make sure the thumb hole is drilled large enough to allow an easy release, and the finger holes drilled to fit more tightly in order to insure the proper release on a hook ball. If you bowl a straight or backup ball, this fact should be told to the driller. Also tell him if you are left-handed because the ring-finger hole is usually drilled a fraction of an inch farther from the thumb hole than the second-finger hole. This is the reason left-handers should not use right-handed balls.

The "pitch" in the bowling ball is also a very important part of the fit. "Pitch" refers to the degree of inclination the finger holes have toward or away from the center of the bowling ball.

The more the finger holes are cut in so that the fingers can approximate a more clenched position when they are inside the ball, the greater the grip

Fig. 9.1  A Bowler's Personal Equipment

feeling the bowler has. The standard for a conventional grip is ⅜-inch pitch above the center of the ball. Too much pitch can curtail one's ability to release the fingers from the ball.

Balls can now be purchased in a variety of colors in addition to the traditional black. To appeal to the ladies' tastes, balls, shoes, and ball bags can be purchased in matching colors and a variety of combinations. The newer plastic balls, while attractive looking, crack or chip more easily and tend to become scratched in brush polishers. Recently, foreign-made bowling balls have appeared in this country at reduced prices. These may not be perfectly round or may have a surface which is too hard or too soft. A ball with a surface which is too hard will tend to skid, while one with a surface too soft will show wear quickly.

## PURCHASE OF BOWLING SHOES

Comfortable and well fitted bowling shoes are another important item to consider for good performance in bowling.

For a right-handed bowler, the right bowling shoe should have a leather tip, rubber sole and heel. The left shoe should have a smooth leather sole for sliding and a rubber heel for "braking." A left-hander's shoes are made in the opposite fashion. There are many styles, colors, and varieties of leather from which to choose.

## BOWLING BAGS

Since bowling balls are quite heavy and awkward to carry, it is almost essential that you purchase a ball bag which also protects the ball from becoming scratched or nicked. (A combination ball and shoe bag is even better.) They can be purchased in leather or imitation leather, canvas or a combination of materials. Make sure the handles are secured firmly because there is constant strain on them from lifting and supporting the heavy weight.

## OTHER EQUIPMENT

Although the ball and shoes are the basic equipment, numerous other items are available to the bowler. There are patented grips to insert in the thumb or finger holes to prevent slippage. Some bowlers feel that bowling gloves give them better control of the balls. Gloves are recommended for persons who do a lot of competitive bowling, or who have soft or sensitive skin and tend to develop blisters easily.

Many bowling establishments offer a complete line of bowling shirts for men and women. When selecting bowling attire, remember the suggestions outlined in chapter 2—dress in good taste with clothes that allow freedom of movement.

# Playing the game

# 10

Once you have learned the fundamental bowling techniques from a competent instructor and have practiced to the extent that you have a reasonable amount of consistency in the delivery of the ball, you may wish to try out your talents in a recreational or competitive situation. If you are not too sure of your own performance and wish to use scores as criteria for taking the initial dive into league competition, you would probably feel more at ease if you were capable of averaging 120 (women) or 140 (men). Studies of the performance of college bowlers indicated that students with these or better averages are in the "intermediate" or "experienced" category, and thus most of them could enjoy league bowling. The studies also showed a difference of approximately 20 pins between averages of men and women in selected groupings of "beginning" and "experienced" bowlers.

## BOWLING OPPORTUNITIES

Students in most of the larger colleges and universities have an excellent opportunity to learn bowling and to compete in intramural leagues right on their own campuses. The modern college student union buildings have included bowling lanes as part of the total campus recreation for students, faculty, and employees. The easiest procedure is to first enroll in a bowling class in the physical education department, learn or review the proper techniques from a qualified instructor, and get acquainted with various types of bowling competition offered by the class. Here you have the advantage of

---

**Assume that your average score is 120; 135; 150. In each case what would
your handicap be?**

---

bowling with people of your own age and ability and with whom you can
become quite well acquainted. This lets you break into competition in a
more relaxed atmosphere.

Next, you may wish to consider entering an intramural or student
union tournament as a member of a fraternity or dormitory team. These
usually are handicap tournaments where, in order to equalize the competition, bowlers are given a handicap.

If there is no opportunity for you to bowl on campus, try a commercial
lane. There are commercial lanes in the near vicinity of most college com-
munities. Many types of leagues or tournaments are in operation both during the winter and in the summer.


## LEAGUE BOWLING

Leagues are established at the request of church groups, commercial and
business groups, industrial organizations, and other occupational groups.
These usually are handicap leagues although most bowling centers have at
least one "scratch" league for the more advanced men and women bowlers.
Organized league bowling is ordinarily sanctioned by the A.B.C. for men,
and the W.I.B.C. for women. Persons bowling in such sanctioned leagues
must pay a small fee to join the A.B.C. or W.I.B.C. and can establish an
official average with the organization.

League teams are made up of four or five (the most common) bowlers,
but two-man teams and mixed bowling are also common. Teams usually
bowl once a week with each team member rolling three lines per series.

To equalize teams with bowlers of varying ability, handicaps are established. There are various methods of computing handicaps; however, two
common practices will be detailed here. One system is based on two-thirds
of the difference between the bowler's present averages and 190. For example, a bowler with an average of 145 would have a handicap of 30 (190
minus 145 is 45; two-thirds of 45 is 30). This handicap may change from
week to week as new scores are averaged in. The second method, recommended by the A.B.C., uses 75 percent of the difference between the bowler's average (over 18-21 games) and a scratch score determined by the participating league. Leagues for men often use a 200 scratch score while leagues
for women frequently use a 180 scratch score. A bowler with a 200 (man)
or a 180 (woman) average is called a "scratch bowler" which indicates that

he doesn't have a handicap. The following table gives the handicap for any participant who has an established average of between 100 and 200:

## HANDICAP TABLE—SCRATCH 200
### 75%

| Average | Handicap | Average | Handicap | Average | Handicap | Average | Handicap |
|---------|----------|---------|----------|---------|----------|---------|----------|
| 199 | 0 | 174 | 19 | 149 | 38 | 124 | 57 |
| 198 | 1 | 173 | 20 | 148 | 39 | 123 | 57 |
| 197 | 2 | 172 | 21 | 147 | 39 | 122 | 58 |
| 196 | 3 | 171 | 21 | 146 | 40 | 121 | 59 |
| 195 | 3 | 170 | 22 | 145 | 41 | 120 | 60 |
| 194 | 4 | 169 | 23 | 144 | 42 | 119 | 60 |
| 193 | 5 | 168 | 24 | 143 | 42 | 118 | 61 |
| 192 | 6 | 167 | 24 | 142 | 43 | 117 | 62 |
| 191 | 6 | 166 | 25 | 141 | 44 | 116 | 63 |
| 190 | 7 | 165 | 26 | 140 | 45 | 115 | 63 |
| 189 | 8 | 164 | 27 | 139 | 45 | 114 | 64 |
| 188 | 9 | 163 | 27 | 138 | 46 | 113 | 65 |
| 187 | 9 | 162 | 28 | 137 | 47 | 112 | 66 |
| 186 | 10 | 161 | 29 | 136 | 48 | 111 | 66 |
| 185 | 11 | 160 | 30 | 135 | 48 | 110 | 67 |
| 184 | 12 | 159 | 30 | 134 | 49 | 109 | 68 |
| 183 | 12 | 158 | 31 | 133 | 50 | 108 | 69 |
| 182 | 13 | 157 | 32 | 132 | 51 | 107 | 69 |
| 181 | 14 | 156 | 33 | 131 | 51 | 106 | 70 |
| 180 | 15 | 155 | 33 | 130 | 52 | 105 | 71 |
| 179 | 15 | 154 | 34 | 129 | 53 | 104 | 72 |
| 178 | 16 | 153 | 35 | 128 | 54 | 103 | 72 |
| 177 | 17 | 152 | 36 | 127 | 54 | 102 | 73 |
| 176 | 18 | 151 | 36 | 126 | 55 | 101 | 74 |
| 175 | 18 | 150 | 37 | 125 | 56 | 100 | 75 |

## HANDICAP TABLE—SCRATCH 180
### 75%

| Average | Handicap | Average | Handicap | Average | Handicap | Average | Handicap |
|---------|----------|---------|----------|---------|----------|---------|----------|
| 179 | 1 | 159 | 16 | 139 | 31 | 119 | 46 |
| 178 | 2 | 158 | 17 | 138 | 32 | 118 | 47 |
| 177 | 2 | 157 | 17 | 137 | 32 | 117 | 47 |
| 176 | 3 | 156 | 18 | 136 | 33 | 116 | 48 |

| Average | Handicap | Average | Handicap | Average | Handicap | Average | Handicap |
|---------|----------|---------|----------|---------|----------|---------|----------|
| 175 | 4 | 155 | 19 | 135 | 34 | 115 | 49 |
| 174 | 5 | 154 | 20 | 134 | 35 | 114 | 50 |
| 173 | 5 | 153 | 20 | 133 | 35 | 113 | 50 |
| 172 | 6 | 152 | 21 | 132 | 36 | 112 | 51 |
| 171 | 7 | 151 | 22 | 131 | 37 | 111 | 52 |
| 170 | 8 | 150 | 23 | 130 | 38 | 110 | 53 |
| 169 | 8 | 149 | 23 | 129 | 38 | 109 | 53 |
| 168 | 9 | 148 | 24 | 128 | 39 | 108 | 54 |
| 167 | 10 | 147 | 25 | 127 | 40 | 107 | 55 |
| 166 | 11 | 146 | 26 | 126 | 41 | 106 | 56 |
| 165 | 11 | 145 | 26 | 125 | 41 | 105 | 56 |
| 164 | 12 | 144 | 27 | 124 | 42 | 104 | 57 |
| 163 | 13 | 143 | 28 | 123 | 43 | 103 | 58 |
| 162 | 14 | 142 | 29 | 122 | 44 | 102 | 59 |
| 161 | 14 | 141 | 29 | 121 | 44 | 101 | 59 |
| 160 | 15 | 140 | 30 | 120 | 45 | 100 | 60 |

### Scoring—and What It Means

A typical score sheet for a handicap league demonstrates how the system enables individuals and teams with different skill ability to compete.

At the beginning of each game, the captain adds the handicaps for his team. The Saints had a total of 110 and the Rockies had a team handicap of 150. The team with the smaller handicap would be the better team of bowlers although the handicap will equalize the teams. At the conclusion of the game, the final scores for the team members are totaled, and to that total is added the team's total handicap. Teams score their final team results on a cumulative basis after the tenth frame rather than waiting until all bowlers have finished the game to total the score. In our example, the Saints won with 716 pins over the Rockies who scored 674 pins.

*Reading the "Marks"*    An indication of the progressive competition between teams during a game is provided by a system of "marking." To indicate the difference in handicaps between the teams, marks are given. Each mark represents ten pins. Four marks, as indicated by the number in the circle on the score sheet, were given to the Rockies to account for the 40-pin difference in team handicaps at the beginning of the game. Subsequently, a running account of the game from frame to frame is recorded by totaling cumulative marks, either strikes or spares (see the center of the score sheet). This system enables the bowlers, by counting team marks, to approximate how close the teams are during any frame.

| TEAMS: SAINTS VS. ROCKIES | | | | | | | | | | | | |
|---|---|---|---|---|---|---|---|---|---|---|---|---|
| NAME | HDCP. | 1 | 2 | 3 | 4 | 5 | 6 | 7 | 8 | 9 | 10 | TOTAL |
| Rich | 44 | 7 1<br>8 | 9 /<br>25 | 7 /<br>41 | 6 2<br>49 | 8 -<br>57 | X<br>75 | 8 -<br>83 | 7 2<br>92 | 8 (0)<br>101 | X 9 /<br>121 | 121 |
| Myers | 37 | 9 -<br>9 | G 9<br>18 | 7 (2)<br>27 | 6 /<br>46 | 9 /<br>66 | X<br>86 | 8 Ø<br>102 | 6 /<br>119 | 7 2<br>128 | 7 -<br>135 | 256 |
| Kob | 29 | X<br>20 | 7 /<br>40 | X<br>58 | 4 4<br>66 | 9 /<br>86 | 8 /<br>102 | 6 3<br>119 | 8 /<br>126 | 7 2<br>135 | 5 / X<br>155 | 411 |
| Miller | 0<br>TOTAL 110 | 9 /<br>20 | X<br>50 | X<br>79 | X<br>99 | 9 /<br>118 | 9 -<br>127 | X<br>146 | 8 1<br>155 | X<br>175 | 5 / X<br>195 | 606 |
| Saints<br>Rockies | (4) | 2/5 | 5/7 | 8/8 | 10/11 | 13/13 | 16/16 | 18/18 | 20/20 | 21/22 | 27/26 | +110<br>716 |
| Locke | 53 | 1 -<br>1 | 4 /<br>21 | X<br>41 | 8 /<br>54 | 3 4<br>61 | 7 1<br>69 | 8 /<br>82 | 3 5<br>90 | 1 8<br>99 | 6 -<br>105 | 105 |
| Tanner | 49 | 6 1<br>7 | 5 2<br>14 | G 5<br>19 | 5 /<br>35 | 6 3<br>44 | 6 /<br>64 | X<br>84 | 9 /<br>103 | 9 /<br>120 | 7 2<br>129 | 234 |
| Koone | 35 | 8 1<br>9 | 8 1<br>18 | 6 3<br>27 | 8 /<br>44 | 7 /<br>64 | X<br>83 | 7 2<br>92 | X<br>111 | 7 2<br>120 | 9 / X<br>140 | 374 |
| Lacey | 13<br>TOTAL 150 | 8 /<br>17 | 7 /<br>36 | 9 -<br>45 | 8 1<br>54 | X<br>74 | 5 /<br>93 | 9 -<br>102 | 6 2<br>110 | 7 /<br>130 | X 8 /<br>150 | 524<br>+150<br>674 |

Fig. 10.1 Sample Score Sheet

For those who want to keep a more accurate running score "good" marks and "negative" marks are tabulated. There are three basic rules to follow in figuring marks:

1. One mark is given for each single strike or spare.
2. Two marks are given for each consecutive strike.

**3.** Marks are *lost* if an individual fails to knock over at least five pins—
   **a.** with the first ball following a spare
   **b.** with the first ball following a multiple strike
   **c.** with both balls in a frame
   **d.** with both balls following a strike

The total number of marks in the first frame would be two (one for the strike and one for the spare). In the second frame, Pat adds a mark but Kay loses a mark since her first ball following her spare got only three pins, so the total number of marks after two frames for this team is two. In the third frame Pat again gets one mark and Kay loses one because she did not total at least five pins in that frame, therefore the total marks after three frames is two. For the fourth frame, Pat gets two marks for his consecutive strike, and Kay gets one for the spare. There was no loss so the total marks through four frames is five.

| | 1 | 2 | 3 | 4 |
|---|---|---|---|---|
| PAT | ☒ | 8 / | ☒ | ☒ |
| KAY | 7 / | 3 6 | 0 3 | 9 / |
| TOTAL MARKS | 2 | 2 | 2 | 5 |

Even though this system of marking is more accurate than the one used on the Sample Score Sheet (fig. 10.1), the final scores may vary as much as forty to fifty pins even though the final mark totals are even. This would occur if one team consistently had a higher pin count on their spares and total pins in a frame.

In addition to handicap leagues, there are opportunities for "open" and "scratch" leagues. In these leagues, there is no restriction on the basis of average, and no handicaps. Teams are credited only with the pins knocked down.

Women's or housewives' leagues and senior citizens' leagues are popular during the morning and early afternoon hours. Junior leagues for boys and girls are available on Saturday mornings or after school. Since most of the evening hours during the week are reserved for league bowling it is always wise to inquire as to the hours the lanes are available for "open bowling," or to phone to find out if it is possible to reserve a lane for practice or for an informal game.

## ADDITIONAL BOWLING EXPERIENCES

If you wish to learn from watching topnotch performers, consult your local bowling establishment or watch the sports page of your newspaper for announcements of exhibition matches by the professional bowlers or leading tournament teams.

Bowling, like golf, has gained in popularity with television audiences to such an extent that not only are the finals of the winter tournaments of the Pro Bowlers Tour, the U.S. Open, and All-Star events televised, but other exciting matches between champions can also be observed on TV Saturdays and Sundays.

There are, in addition, many films available on loan or rental basis from the leading bowling equipment companies and other distributors. A list of these plus supplemental reading on bowling can be found in the selected references.

Of special interest are several variations of bowling or novelty events that, besides being fun for parties and diversions from regular league play, are also excellent for sharpening the bowling eye. These include the following games, all of which make use of standard equipment and lanes.

*Blind Bowling.* A wire strung with a curtain is hung above the lane, about halfway down, to block the bowler's view of the pins. Regular scoring is used and the automatic pin machines show the spare setups remaining. Excellent practice for spot bowling.

*Cocked Hat.* Set up pins 3-7-10 (for right-handers) or 2-7-10 (for left-handers). Use two balls per frame as in regular bowling and the scoring is similar except strikes and spares score only three instead of ten points.

*Cocked Hat and Feather.* Set up pins 1-3-7-10 or 1-2-7-10 and play in the same manner as in the foregoing.

The 1-5-7-10 setup can also be used—the object being to leave the 5 pin standing. If it should be upset, there is no score in that frame. Both games are good practice for spare bowling but are admittedly difficult to arrange with automatic pinsetters.

*Headpin.* Bowler rolls only one ball per frame, but scores nothing unless the headpin goes down. Score as in regular bowling, but of course there are no spares.

*Rotation.* If no red pin is available, the various numbered pins can be used as the red pin or "IT" pin. Start with #1 on first ball, #2 on second

Have you found out what league play is open to you in your locality?—
which tournaments are sponsored?—when the alleys have open bowling
hours?

ball, etc. Bowler rolls only one ball per frame. Scored as the foregoing in
that the bowler receives nothing unless the red pin or the particular
pin he is shooting for also goes down.

*Scotch Doubles.* A partnership game, usually mixed doubles wherein part-
ners roll every other ball throughout the line. Regular scoring is used.
A variation in the game allows for a partner to roll the next ball provided he or she has made a strike or a spare on the previous ball. The
latter form of the game is more enjoyable for men bowlers who then
have more chances to roll strikes than if they roll in second position
only and so have to do mostly spare bowling.

This book has attempted to give you a point of reference or a basis for
building good bowling habits. Each bowler will develop his own style and
methods for practice through discovering his best working pace. Discover
it, stay with it, and enjoy a fascinating game in the process.

# Selected references

American Bowling Congress (ABC). *History of Bowling*. Milwaukee, Wis.: American Bowling Congress. 1959.

American Machine and Foundry (AMF). *Bowling Instructors' Manual*. 1962.

ARCHIBALD, JOHN J. *Bowling for Boys and Girls*. Chicago: Follett Publishing Co. 1963.

BELLISIMO, LOU and NEAL, LARRY. *Bowling*. Englewood Cliffs, N.J.: Prentice-Hall, Inc., 1971.

BROER, MARION R. *Efficiency of Human Movement*. 3d ed. Philadelphia: W. B. Saunders Company, 1973.

CARTER; NAGY; LADEWIG; FAZIO; and NORRIS. *The Complete Guide to Better Bowling*. New York: Maco Magazine Corp., 1959.

CASADY, DONALD, and LIBA, MARIA. *Beginning Bowling*. Belmont Calif.: Wadsworth Publishing Co., 1962.

FALCARO, JOE, and GOODMAN, MURRAY. *Bowling for All*. Rev. ed. New York: Ronald Press, 1966.

KIDWELL, KATHRO, and SMITH, PAUL, JR. *Bowling Analyzed*. Dubuque, Iowa: Wm. C. Brown Company Publishers, 1960.

MACKEY, RICHARD T. *Bowling*. Palo Alto, Calif.: National Press Books, 1974.

Nation Association for Girls and Women's Sports. *Bowling, Fencing and Golf Guide*. Washington, D.C.: American Alliance for Health, Physical Education and Recreation. (Published at even-year intervals.)

TAYLOR, DAWSON. *The Secret of Bowling Strikes*. New York: A. S. Barnes and Co., 1960.

WILMAN, JOE. *Better Bowling*. New York: Ronald Press, 1953.

Women's International Bowling Congress, Inc. (W.I.B.C.). *League Rule Book*. Columbus, Ohio: Women's International Bowling Congress, Inc. (Published annually.)

Have you watched bowling on television and studied the pin action and ball deflection in the slow-motion sequences?

## NATIONAL BOWLING PERIODICALS

Bowling Magazine. 1572 E. Capitol Drive, Milwaukee, Wis. 53211.
The National Bowlers Journal & Billiard Review. 1825 No. Lincoln Plaza, Chicago, Ill. 60614.
The Bowling Proprietor. 375 West Higgins Rd., Hoffman Estates, Ill. 60172.
The Woman Bowler. 386 So. Fourth St., Columbus, Ohio 43215.

## FILMS

Beginning Bowling. 1962. Slidefilm, 35 mm., 60 min., sd., color. (2)
Bowling Aces; Set 'Em Up; Strikes and Spares. 16 mm., 9, 10, and 12 min., b&w. (5)
Bowling Fundamentals; Striking Champions. 16 mm., 15 and 12 min., b&w. (5)
Learn to Bowl Series (National Bowling Council). 1973. Sound Slidefilm: (4)

| | |
|---|---|
| "Let It Happen" | "Playing Lanes" |
| "Watch It Happen" | "The Release" |
| "Put It All Together" | "Building on Fundamentals" |
| "Strikes and Spares" | "Think It Through" |
| "Personal Adjustments" | |

Let's Go Bowling. 16 mm., 30 min., sd., b&w. (3)
Tenpin Showcase. 1961. 16 mm., 18 min., sd., b&w. (1)

## Film Distributors

(1)  AMF Pinspotters, Inc., Jericho Turnpike, Westbury, L. I., N.Y.; 6500 N. Lincoln, Chicago, Ill.
(2)  Athletic Institute, Merchandise Mart, Room 805, Chicago, Ill. 60654.
(3)  Bowling Proprietors Association of America, 111 S. Washington, Park Ridge, Ill.
(4)  Richard Manufacturing Company, Van Nuys, Calif.
(5)  ROA's Films, 1696 North Astor St., Milwaukee, Wis.

# Appendix:
# Questions and answers

TRUE OR FALSE

T  f    1. A line consists of 10 frames. (p. 57)
T  f    2. A strike in the tenth frame entitles the bowler to two more balls. (p. 58)
t  F    3. A frame consists of bowling two balls. (p. 57)
T  f    4. A split is recorded thus: ⦏0⦎ (p. 57)
t  F    5. The recommended point of aim is the 1 and 3 pins. (p. 25)
t  F    6. If bowlers on adjoining lanes are ready to start their approaches at the same time, the bowler on the left is given the courtesy of bowling first. (p. 62)
t  F    7. On a four-step delivery, the first three steps should be longer than the fourth. (p. 17)
T  f    8. The Brooklyn pocket is the 1-2 pocket. (p. 53)
t  F    9. Crossing the foul line when bowling voids any score you receive in that frame. (p. 58)
t  F  10. A spare is recorded with an: ⦇X⦈ (p. 58)
T  f  11. To pick up the #7 pin, a bowler should move the starting position slightly right, and the point of aim to the left. (p. 29)
t  F  12. Pulling the arm across the body after releasing the ball is called "side-wheeling." (p. 39, 40)
t  F  13. A ball breaking to the right down the alley is a "hook" ball. (p. 54)
T  f  14. As a general rule, roll spares at cross angles. (p. 26)
t  F  15. To pick up the #2, #4, and #8 pins, roll the ball from the left side of the alley. (p. 30)
t  F  16. The spot aiming technique is best for bowlers using a straight ball; the pin technique is used most by bowlers using a hook or curve. (p. 22)
T  f  17. The position of the hand and wrist for the hook delivery is that of the normal handshake. (p. 13)
t  F  18. In the four-step delivery the ball is pushed away from the body on the second step. (p. 15)
T  f  19. Pins knocked down by another pin rebounding in play from the side partition or rear cushion are counted as pins down. (p. 60)
t  F  20. Most experts use the pin technique because the pins are seen more easily than the spot. (p. 22)

t  F   21. A spare is marked with a horizontal dash (—) in the appropriate box. (p. 58)

t  F   22. After the release, a bowler should lean away from the foul line and balance by stepping on the right foot. (p. 19)

t  F   23. To pick up the #6 and #10 pins, a bowler releases the ball from the right side of the alley. (p. 32)

T  f   24. To knock down the #1, #3, and #5 pins, roll from the right side of the alley. (p. 28)

T  f   25. Pins knocked down by a ball that leaves the alley prior to hitting the pins shall not count. (p. 61)

T  f   26. A foul is charged against a player if he steps over the foul detecting device to avoid fouling. (p. 60)

T  f   27. Between balls a bowler should step to the rear of the approach. (p. 63)

t  F   28. An error is recorded as a diagonal line when scoring: ☑ (p. 57)

t  F   29. Spot bowling is best accomplished by watching the release spot at the foul line. (p. 23)

T  f   30. In using a four-step approach, a bowler starts with the right foot. (p. 15)

T  f   31. Lanes which have just been cleaned and oiled are usually fast and cut down the amount of hook on the ball. (p. 5)

t  F   32. A bowler's primary objective is to develop maximum speed of the ball in order to attain the highest pin count. (p. 6)

t  F   33. Regulation bowling balls range in weight from 10 to 20 pounds. (p. 5)

t  F   34. In the conventional grip, the fingers and thumb are inserted in the holes to the first joint. (p. 8)

T  f   35. In most situations after a split occurs, the average bowler should "play it safe" and attempt to get one pin of two, or two of three or four. (p. 36)

T  f   36. The Dutch are responsible for introducing bowling in America in 1626. (p. 52)

t  F   37. Since its early development in this country, bowling has always been considered a clean and wholesome activity for American youth. (p. 53)

t  F   38. Most women should learn to bowl with a 15 or 16 pound ball. (p. 65)

T  f   39. A bowler with a great amount of hook should select a point of aim more to the right of the second arrow. (p. 24)

t  F   40. A "backup" style of delivery is recommended for left-handed bowlers. (p. 34)

T  f   41. In spare bowling, if all else is forgotten, plan on hitting the pin closest to you to get your spare. (p. 26)

T  f   42. When lifting a ball from the rack or turntable, the ball should be lifted with both hands placed on the sides of the ball, away from other oncoming balls. (p. 8)

T  f   43. In delivering a hook ball, a bowler should feel the thumb release first, then the fingers. (p. 18)

t  F   44. The letters A.B.C. refer to the national bowling organization called the Allied Bowling Council. (p. 54)

T  f   45. To remedy a ball crossing over to the Brooklyn side, a bowler may move his starting position to his left and cut down his angle of roll. (p. 25)

T  f   46. If a bowler wishes to increase the velocity of his ball, the ball can be held higher at chest or chin level at the starting position. (p. 39)

t  F   47. The release point at the foul line should be in the vicinity of the center dot. (p. 24)

t  F   48. In learning to develop the proper sense of timing in the four-step approach, a bowler should practice the step pattern first, then fit the arm swing pattern to the step pattern. (p. 11)

t  F   49. "Taps" are the result of poor ball action. (p. 32)

T  f   50. A split occurs when a bowler's first ball hits too "high" on the headpin. (p. 25)

| | | | |
|---|---|---|---|
| t | F | 51. | When a bowler bowls out of turn, he is penalized the pins he knocked down in that frame. (p. 61) |
| t | F | 52. | "Dead wood" refers to pins which are cracked or damaged. (p. 61) |
| T | f | 53. | "Pitch" refers to the degree of inclination the finger holes have toward the center of the ball. (p. 54) |
| T | f | 54. | Bowling shoes are a necessity for efficient performance because the right shoe has a leather tip, rubber sole and heel; whereas, the left shoe has a smooth leather sole. (p. 67) |
| T | f | 55. | A male bowler whose average is 157 would have a handicap of 22 according to the more common handicapping procedures. (p. 69) |
| t | F | 56. | "Scotch doubles" is a partnership game where partners roll every other frame throughout the line. (p. 75) |
| t | F | 57. | For the proper starting position in the four-step approach most of the body weight is on the right foot to act as a reminder that the first step should be taken on the left foot. (p. 11) |
| T | f | 58. | The straight ball delivery requires less hand and wrist strength than the hook ball delivery. (p. 20) |
| t | F | 59. | The term "straight ball" refers to the line the ball rolls from foul line to pins. (p. 20) |
| T | f | 60. | "Straight balls" should be delivered from the right side of the lane. (p. 20) |
| T | f | 61. | In checking a well-balanced follow-through position at the foul line, the toe and knee of the left leg should form a vertical line with the shoulders. (p. 19) |
| t | F | 62. | To add more hook there should be more turn over of the right hand at release. (p. 41) |
| T | f | 63. | It is possible to roll a score of 180 without ever making a strike. (p. 26) |
| t | F | 64. | Most expert bowlers spot bowl the first ball and pin bowl the second ball. (p. 22) |
| t | F | 65. | A bowler who is consistently right of his spot often rolls the ball too soon before his fourth step is completed. (p. 41) |

66. | | X | | X | 3-6 | 9 |
    | 100 | | | | 151 |

67. | | X | | X | 3-0 | 3 |
    | 10 | | | | 49 |

68. | | ◿ | | X | 5-3 | 8 |
    | 76 | | | | 122 |

69. | | X | | X | | X | 4-5 | 9 |
    | 60 | | | | | 142 |

70. | | X | ◿ | X | 2-5 | 7 |
    | 100 | | | | 164 |

71. | | ◺ | 4-6 | ◺ | 3-5 | 8 |
    | 0 | | | | 35 |

72. | 8 | 9 | 10 | | |
    | ◿ | X | X | X |
    | 170 | 220 | | |

73. | 9 | 10 | | |
    | X | 3 | 7 |
    | 136 | 156 | |

74. | 9 | 10 | | |
    | X | 0 | 9 |
    | 144 | 163 | |

75. | | X | | X | 7 | |
    | 152 | | 196 | |

## MATCHING

| | | | | |
|---|---|---|---|---|
| (17) | 76. | railroad (p. 55) | 1. | 7-10 |
| (16) | 77. | error (p. 57) | 2. | thumb at 12 o'clock |
| (13) | 78. | middle spare (p. 28) | 3. | Kegler |
| (25) | 79. | Brooklyn hit (p. 53) | 4. | 3-6-10 |
| (18) | 80. | left-side spare (p. 29) | 5. | cherry |
| (11) | 81. | backup ball (p. 34) | 6. | open |
| (32) | 82. | lane (p. 54) | 7. | bolla |
| ( 1) | 83. | bedposts (p. 55) | 8. | lemon |
| (36) | 84. | hook ball (p. 18) | 9. | 2-4-5-8 |
| (12) | 85. | sleeper (p. 55) | 10. | range finder |
| ( 9) | 86. | bucket (p. 55) | 11. | thumb at 1 o'clock |
| (27) | 87. | baby split (p. 55) | 12. | a hidden pin |
| ( 6) | 88. | a frame without a mark (p. 57) | 13. | 5-9 |
| ( 5) | 89. | chopping off front pin (p. 55) | 14. | turkey |
| (10) | 90. | spot bowling (p. 55) | 15. | bulla |
| (19) | 91. | releasing ball noisily beyond foul line (p. 54) | 16. | blow |
| ( 2) | 92. | straight ball (p. 14) | 17. | split |
| ( 7) | 93. | ancient Saxon term for "bowl" (p. 50) | 18. | 4-7-8 |
| (14) | 94. | three strikes in a row (p. 59) | 19. | loft |
| ( 4) | 95. | right-side spare (p. 31) | 20. | boule |
| (31) | 96. | distance between holes on ball (p. 53) | 21. | eagle |
| (24) | 97. | famous male bowler of early Europe (p. 51) | 22. | thumb at 8 o'clock |
| (33) | 98. | strike or spare (p. 56) | 23. | chicken |
| (35) | 99. | using actual scores in competition (p. 56) | 24. | Martin Luther |
| (37) | 100. | 2 strikes in a row (p. 56) | 25. | 1-2 pocket |
| | | | 26. | Charlemagne |
| | | | 27. | 2-7 |
| | | | 28. | thumb at 3 o'clock |
| | | | 29. | lob |
| | | | 30. | thumb at 7 o'clock |
| | | | 31. | bridge |
| | | | 32. | alley |
| | | | 33. | mark |
| | | | 34. | George V |
| | | | 35. | scratch |
| | | | 36. | thumb at 10 o'clock |
| | | | 37. | double |

## ANSWERS TO EVALUATION QUESTIONS

*No answer

| Page | Answer and Page Reference |
|---|---|
| 18 | Hook. (p. 18) |
| 16 | * |
| 25 | * |
| 42 | * |
| 52 | Brooklyn. p. 53. Caused by hitting to left on headpin, 1-2 instead of 1-3 pocket. |

1. Timing too fast—forcing the ball on delivery.
2. Fingers release too late.

58

| 1 | 2 | 3 | 4 | 5 | 6 | 7 | 8 | 9 | 10 | Total |
|---|---|---|---|---|---|---|---|---|---|---|
| 6 | 7 2 | | | | 9 | F | 1 | 8 1 9 | | |
| 17 | 26 | 56 | 85 | 104 | 113 | 133 | 152 | 161 | 181 | 181 |

Ch. 7

# Index

Petrie, Sir F., 50
Physical education, 2, 68
Pin action, 47, 48
Pin fall, 60, 61
 illegal, 61
 legal, 60
Pitch, 54, 66
Pocket, 23, 25, 26, 34, 35, 39, 47, 55

Rack, 63, 64
Railroad, 36, 55
Range finder, 5, 25
Relaxation, 11
Replacement of pins, 61
Return, 8, 55
Rogers, Dr. M., 50
Rotation, 74
Rules, 57
 fouls, 58
Running lanes, 35, 55

Score, 1, 57, 72
Scratch, 56
Scratch bowler, 54, 69
Scotch doubles, 75
Semiroller, 33
Semispinner, 33
"Shadow bowling," 42
"Sidewheeling," 40
Skills:
 approach, 11, 12, 13
 backswing, 14, 15, 16, 39, 48
 basic, 8
 "check points," 19
 follow-through, 18, 19, 20, 46, 47
 forward swing, 17, 18, 21, 48
 grip, 7, 9, 11, 20, 37
 learning of, 6
 picking up ball, 8
 push-away, 14, 15, 48
 stance, 10, 19
 swing patterns, 14, 15, 37, 38, 48

"Sleeper," 28, 55
Slide, 17, 18, 46
Span, 9, 54
Spares, 26, 27, 28, 56, 57, 58
 "covering," 28
 definition of, 26, 56
 left side, 28, 29
 middle, 28, 29
 picking up, 26, 27
 right side, 30, 31
 scoring of, 57, 58
Spin, 20, 33, 34, 47
Splits, 25, 31, 32, 55, 56
 baby, 55
 scoring of, 57
Spot, 19, 23, 25, 26, 55
Starting position, 10, 24, 28
Steal, 56
Step pattern, 15
Straight ball, 14, 20, 28, 33
Strategy, 35
Strike, 22, 28, 36, 56, 57, 58
Strike out, 56
Substitute, 60

Taps, 32, 55
Target, 10, 18, 19, 23, 24
Team, 1, 35, 60, 62, 68, 69
Television, 3, 41, 74
Terminology, 53
Three quarter roller, 33
Thumb, 8, 13, 14, 18, 20, 25, 33, 47, 66
Timing, 15, 17, 18, 39
Track, 33, 34
Turkey, 56, 59

Values, 1-2

Warm-ups, 37
Washout, 55
Women's International Bowling Congress,
 3, 53, 54, 59, 69
Working ball, 54